Archaeology

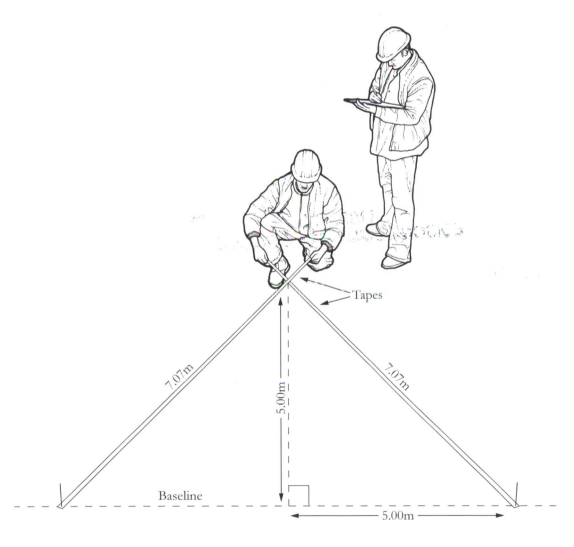

Tapes

7.07m 7.07m

5.00m

Baseline

5.00m

Paul Wilkinson

Archaeopress
Gordon House
276 Banbury Road
Oxford
OX2 7ED

bar@archaeopress.com
www.archaeopress.com

Archaeology
What it is, where it is, and how to do it

ISBN 978 1 905739 00 4

Printed in England by Caric Press

Archaeology

What it is, where it is, and how to do it

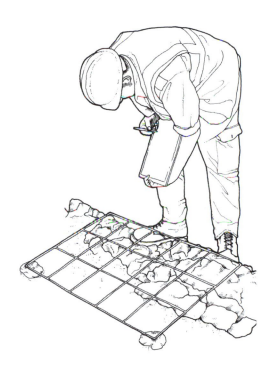

Paul Wilkinson

The thrill of archaeology: Pottery sherds, one of the building blocks of field archaeology which help to identify and date sites.
The study of pottery is important for three reasons. Firstly, to date sites and contexts when other datable objects are lacking; secondly, pottery provides information about trade and distribution; thirdly, it furthers the understanding of ceramics themselves.

This book could not have been written without the help and advice of many archaeologists and tutors of the Kent Archaeological Field School.

In particular:
The specialists of the Museum of London, MoLSS and MoLAS
Archaeologists of English Heritage
Paul Cuming, Sites and Monuments Record Manager, Kent County Council
Damian Grady, Senior Investigator, Aerial Survey, English Heritage
Michael Lewis, Deputy Head of Portable Antiquities, British Museum
Andy Payne, Archaeometry Branch, English Heritage
Peter Rowsome, Senior Manager, MoLSS
Ges Moody, Emma Boast, Trust for Thanet Archaeology
Geoff Morley, archaeologist
Dr Robert Prescott, Institute of Maritime Studies, Univerity of St Andrews,
Catherine Wilkinson, archaeologist
Artwork by Will Foster, Monitos.art@virgin.net

Contents

List of Figures

The potential of archaeology is shown in this wonderful estate map of part of the city of Gloucester. The city walls and the tidal mill are shown functioning in the sixteenth century.
These structures are now Heritage Sites whilst the roofless buildings, already in ruins on the map, have now disappeared, but they could survive below the turf as buried archaeology.

INTRODUCTION

This book has been written as a practical introduction on the investigation of the material remains of the past which can be interpreted with contemporary historical and literary evidence. The book also explains where to find this evidence and what to do next. Every archaeological field activity needs to be recorded. If it is not, the opportunity to provide evidence and understanding of our past is lost and in many cases the evidence is forgotten.

Our landscape, both rural and urban, is one of the most important historical documents that we have, and we can unravel it by observation, investigation and recording. But we need to survey and record our archaeological activities in the field to a standard which is acceptable to the profession today. It is also worth remembering that the great archaeologist, Sir Mortimer Wheeler, once said 'a site is not discovered until it is published'.

It is well to remember that archaeology in the field is not to be carried out just for its own sake, but as a means to create new knowledge, to revise theory and to interpret existing evidence in new ways. Although this book can serve to provide a basic explanation of archaeological practice it is worth remembering that every facet of this wonderful, exciting discipline will need careful study and lots of experience - which will come in time.

All intrusive archaeological investigations should be supervised by a registered Member of the Institute of Field Archaeologists (MIFA), who will maintain standards. The IFA was established to define and maintain proper professional standards. All archaeologists undertaking field investigations must have adequate insurance; advice is available from the IFA (tel: 0118 378 6446, admin@archaeologists.net) or the Council of British Archaeology (CBA), tel: 01904 671417, admin@britarch.ac.uk.

Archaeology courses are held at educational establishments across the country. But many students do find it difficult to gain access to practical courses and training excavations. Do consult the CBA or 'Current Archaeology', or try my own organisation, the Kent Archaeological Field School (KAFS). Our courses cover all aspects of archaeology and are suitable for anyone with an interest in archaeology. Previous experience is unnecessary and beginners are welcome. Training excavations are fully supervised by professional archaeologists and are structured as taught courses. The KAFS operates a membership scheme, and benefits include subscription to the *Practical Archaeology* magazine and priority booking. Details of courses and membership forms can be found on our website: www.kafs.co.uk; or tel: 01795 532548; or email: info.kafs.co.uk.

Dr Paul Wilkinson

CHAPTER ONE: DOCUMENTARY SOURCES

'The English landscape itself, to those who know how to read it aright, is the richest historical record we possess'
(The Making of the English Landscape, W.G. Hoskins, 1955).

As a preparation for archaeological work, it is essential to research the history of the particular site that you are interested in. Professional archaeologists usually work within Planning Policy Guidance 16 (PPG 16) and related legislation, which entails the production of environmental impact reports which derive from EEC law, pre-application desk-top studies and desk-based assessments. Most counties now have a Sites and Monuments Record (SMR) that can be consulted. Enquiries will be answered by an Archaeological Officer whose task it is to administer this archaeological record. The SMR, now known as the Historic Environment Record (HER), although not always up to date, will usually contain recorded information about a particular site and list any known archaeological activity on that site. It will tell you if your site is known or listed as a Scheduled Monument. It will list known historical references, visits by Archaeological Field Officers and casual finds made by archaeologists and members of the public. Any archaeological investigation known to have taken place on that site will also be recorded. Access to the SMR over the internet is becoming increasingly common. It would also be worthwhile contacting the county curatorial team who may have more up-to-date information on any particular archaeological site.

Another good source for any archaeological investigation is the National Monuments Record (NMR), part of English Heritage. If you contact the NMR they will provide a Local Studies Resources Pack for a small fee. It will usually include three A3 aerial photographs and the National Monuments Record database printouts

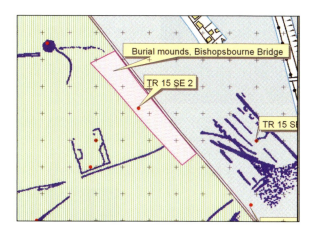

Fig 1 The SMR data around Star Hill at Bridge. The pink area TR 25 NW 14 is the Scheduled Monument Site of an Anglo-Saxon cemetery.

for your particular enquiry. The NMR holds over ten million items, which relate to England's buildings and archaeological sites. In the collections are aerial photographs of all parts of England, archaeological records of England compiled by the Ordnance Survey and former RCHME, and a national database of listed historic buildings and measured drawings of buildings and monuments. The collections are stored at the National Monuments Record Centre (NMRC) in Swindon and can be consulted in the public search rooms; tel: 01793 414660; e-mail: nmrinfo@english-heritage.org.uk.

There is a vast amount of documentary local history material available for study at your local library, the County Record Office, the National Archives (formerly the Public Record Office) at Kew, the British Library at Euston and other specialist libraries and archives. Documents that can give good topographical detail, such as perambulations, surveys and manorial court rolls, should be consulted, and if they are of interest, transcribed and copied. Some documents may include topographic sketch maps, such as the legal papers of land disputes, which may have maps attached highlighting landmarks and field boundaries. Other useful areas of research are museum archaeological archives and collections, the Victoria County Histories, Pevsner's Buildings of England and also unpublished diaries and manuscripts of the site and its locality. Some of these were written by learned gentlemen and retired military officers who were interested in archaeology and kept journals of finds in their parish or district.

Local newspaper archives need to be consulted. Archaeological finds may have been reported in the local press but not recorded by the county archaeological society. Most counties have an archaeological society that usually publishes a book every year containing reports of excavations, discoveries and local finds. The Society of Antiquaries and other august bodies

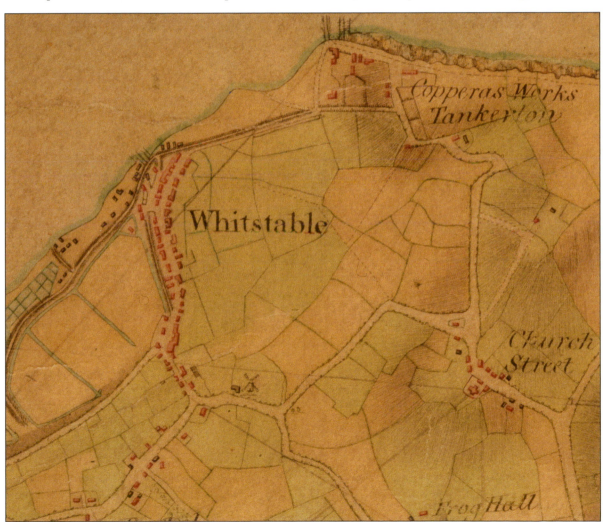

Fig 2 OS Surveyors drawing of Whitstable in 1798. Of interest are the fishermen's huts on the foreshore and the Copperas Houses excavated by Tim Allen in 2003. The buildings shown in red are domestic houses and shops whilst the buildings in black are commercial premises, fishermen's store huts and boat sheds.

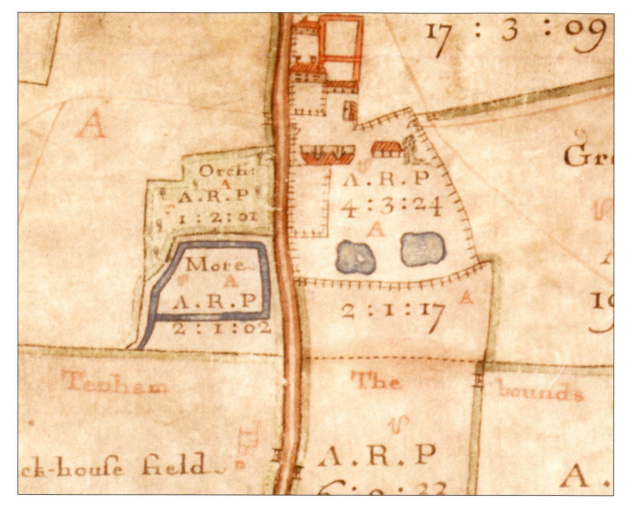

Fig 3 Estate map of Pigeon House Field in Teynham, Kent. Drawn for Lord Teynham in 1706. The map contains a plethora of fascinating information (all of the fields are measured in acres, rods and perches) and shows buildings long disappeared, including a previously unknown moated manor house site. The dotted line running across the map, "The bounds" is probably a late Roman bank and ditch some 22km long.

publish journals that are a mine of information on British archaeology. Most societies have a library open to the public where their book and document collection can be consulted and photocopied. Also the Portable Antiquities Scheme find's database (www.finds.org.uk or http://ads.ahds.ac.uk/heirport) is a valuable documentary source for artefact distribution and artefact typology.

Maps

Maps can be used as historical evidence, and because it generally takes some time to survey and draw a map, it is likely to be an accurate topographic depiction of the locality drawn. However, questions need to be asked on its topographic accuracy. For instance, early 19th-century Ordnance Survey county maps show fields which are usually grossly simplified and distorted, whereas estate maps of two centuries earlier will normally show field boundaries and topographic features correctly drawn because they were made to be accurate. It is essential to gauge the accuracy of early maps by comparing them with a modern Ordnance Survey map or, in the field, against the actual features. It is wise to remember that maps were drawn for a purpose by their originator. Information on

Documentary Sources

Ordnance Survey historic and modern maps can be accessed on the internet: www.ordnancesurvey.co.uk. If a map does not show a particular feature, that does not mean it was not there, just that it may not have been considered important enough to be included. Absence of evidence is not evidence of absence.

Prior to the Ordnance Survey being established in 1791, the most useful corpus of surviving maps is the estate map. About 30,000 maps survive in the public collections; hundreds, if not thousands more are to be found in the private papers of large estates, or still hanging on the walls of grand estate houses, and even in their estate or solicitor's offices.

Estate maps normally show a single landowner's holdings, sometimes a single farm, but more often than not an estate with numerous farms spreading over one or more parishes. The estate map usually shows individual fields, walls, gates, lanes, water courses and rivers. The areas of fields will be in acres, rods and perches. Most estate maps are on a large scale, which enabled small features to be drawn with some accuracy. Field names are itemised. These names can indicate past usage or buried archaeology. 'Blacklands', for instance, can suggest a Roman villa, such as those found at Faversham in Kent and Shapwick in Somerset. 'Wickham' or 'Wycham Field' could suggest a lost Roman settlement and 'Street Field' may refer to the route of a a lost Roman road, whilst 'Mote' can indicate the site of an unknown moated manor house dating from the medieval period (Fig 3). For further information on place names read the excellent books on the subject by Dr Margaret Gelling, past President of the English Place-Name Society.

Fig 4, 5 Comparison between an estate map of 1623 and a map of 2004. Deerton Street, west of Faversham, is the site of a Roman villa found by the author through field-walking. It had its surrounding fields measured out in Roman 'actus quadratus' of 120 sq. ft. The house plots shown on both maps are measured not in Anglo-Saxon feet, but German feet of 335mm, considerably larger than the Roman prototype. These early medieval plots have survived into the twenty-first century with little alteration.

Pre-Ordnance Survey maps abound with interesting features; the 16th-century map of Kent by Lambarde shows the entire chain of early warning beacons whilst the 18th-century Andrews, Drury & Herbert map of Kent shows that the ancient Roman road now called Watling Street was then referred to as 'Green Street', no doubt because of the grass growing on the unused surface of the Roman road (Fig 8).

Town plans

One of the earliest town plans to be used by archaeologists is a Roman marble map of Rome which dates back to the 2nd century. It is sometimes possible to see the full extent of a building being excavated in Rome by referring

to the fragments that still survive from this wonderful antique marble map.

Closer to home, it is possible to name lost Roman settlements in Britain discovered by archaeologists by referring to the Antonine Itinerary, a Roman road itinerary dating from the late 2nd century. Archaeologists in London, like their Rome counterparts, regularly refer to early town maps of London. Norden's plan of 1593, Leake's of 1667 and Rocque's map of 1746 are all used by archaeologists. Other towns also have early maps; some, such as the map of Faversham by Edward Jacob (1774), indicate a number of archaeological sites. In Faversham's case the map shows the government-owned

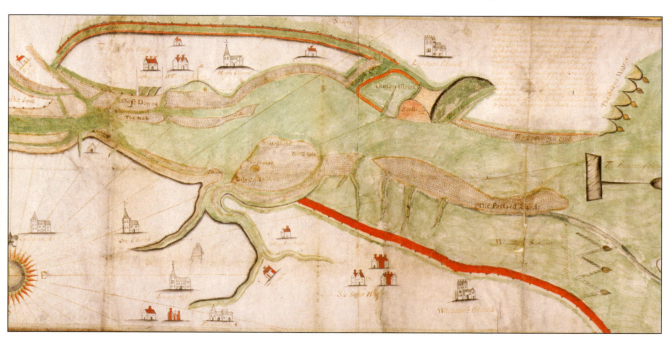

Fig 6 Seventeenth century map of the fishing grounds of the Faversham Oyster Company, the oldest company in the world according to the Guinness Book of Records. The map, painted on vellum shows a tremendous amount of topographic detail, some of it now lost in the landscape.

Fig 7 Map of the beacons in Kent drawn by Lambarde in the sixteenth century. Lambarde actually visited the beacon sites to ensure he had the correct line of site to the other beacons.

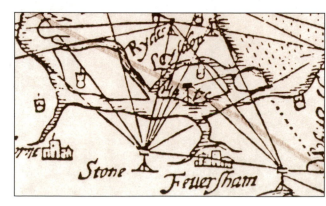

Fig 8 Map by Andrews, Drury & Herbert, 1769 of Watling Street in North Kent. The name Green Street, situated by the 44th milestone, may refer to the medieval disused state of the Roman road overgrown with grass whilst the place-name 'Bapchild' just to the west of Green Street is a very early Saxon habitation name which means 'chattering spring'.

gunpowder works, the first such establishment in England, which dates back to the sixteenth century.

Ordnance Survey maps

Ordnance Survey maps were first drawn when the Board of Ordnance began a military survey of England in 1791, following the alarm over the lack of good military maps available to counter the threat of invasion by Napoleon. By 1797 survey work in Kent by two military survey teams was in hand. The final engraved map of Kent to a scale of 1 inch to a mile was published in 1801. The Ordnance Survey Surveyors' Drawings were surveyed to

Fig 9 John Rocque's map of 1746 shows in exact detail the urban topography of eighteenth-century London. It took over nine years to complete. The scale Rocque used was 26 in. to the mile.

Fig 10 This sixteenth-century map of Faversham shows a palisade surrounding the probable Anglo-Saxon centre of Faversham. The tidal race and over-flow can be seen of the tidal mill called Flood Mill which is itemised in the Domesday Book. The timber-framed buildings are correctly coloured, tiled and not thatched and show the oak timbers in their natural state although the use of brick is shown in chimney construction.

Fig 11 The map detail (right) was painted by Edward Jacob in about 1760 and shows the extent of the town of Faversham. The town still retained its medieval layout but was about to change with the coming of the Industrial Revolution.
The portion illustrated here is of Standard Key and the amount of detail is good when compared to the later engraved copy illustrated below.

Fig 12 Edward Jacob published in 1774 a 'History of Faversham' and also provided a painted map dedicated to 'The Mayor, Jurats and Commonalty' (left). The map was later engraved by Hilton (below) in 1780 to a smaller scale and shows in lesser detail the creek and waterfront of the town. Of particular interest is the overall creek topographic detail which was completely altered by Victorian port engineers and developers.

different scales in different areas. The 6 inch to 1 mile was restricted to parts of Kent (Fig 13), the Isle of Wight and an area around Plymouth.

For archaeological work it is desirable to study the original field drawings on which the engravings were based; they are to be found in the British Library Map Room. Try and study the original field drawings, not the black and white photocopies. On the original drawings colour is used to enhance the features: pasture is painted green, arable is in brown, water courses and rivers blue, habitable houses in red and farm buildings in black. The large-scale, 6-inch drawings show a tremendous amount of topographic detail. Fields are accurately drawn with boundaries showing, as on occasion are individual trees. The survey of Kent was engraved by private contractors to the smaller scale of 1 inch to the mile and issued as a county map (Fig 14) in 1801. The map was an important milestone, being based entirely on surveys prepared by officers of the Board of Ordnance. In the words of Sir Charles Close, the Ordnance Survey historian, the 1801 map of Kent was 'the first Ordnance map'.

In 1836, the Tithe Commutation Act resulted in surveys on which were based large-scale maps for

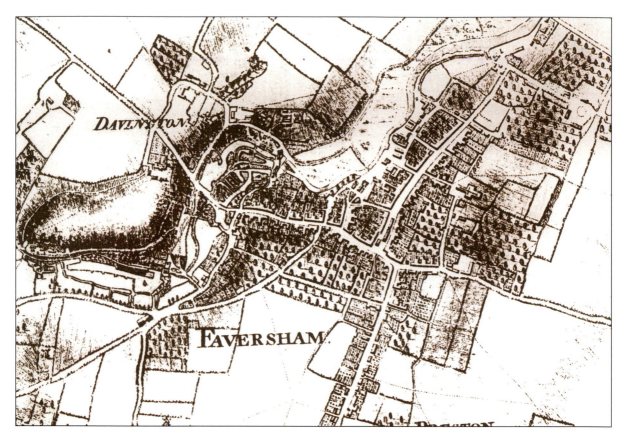

Fig 13 (top) The c.1789 OS surveyors' field drawings of Faversham show in detail the pre-industrial town surveyed for the first time correctly and using survey methods still in use today. The scale used was 6 inches to the mile, and at this scale fields and roads are correct in scale, size and detail.

Fig 14 In 1801 the Board of Ordnance published the first large scale county map based on the surveyors' drawing of c.1789. This portion of the County map of Kent shows the area around the River Medway at Rochester including the forts guarding the Royal Dockyard at Chatham.

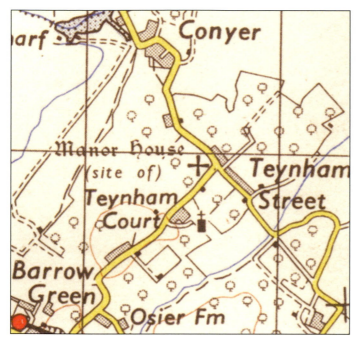

Fig 15 The 1:25,000 scale 1932 OS map of Teynham in Kent showing the lost site of the Archbishop's Palace, marked 'Manor house' and confirmed by archaeological investigation by the Kent Archaeological Field School. To the south is 'Barrow Green' the site of Bronze-Age burial mounds or barrows now destroyed by ploughing. Osier farm is named after the extensive cultivation of willows on the farm to make baskets for the agricultural and fishing industries.

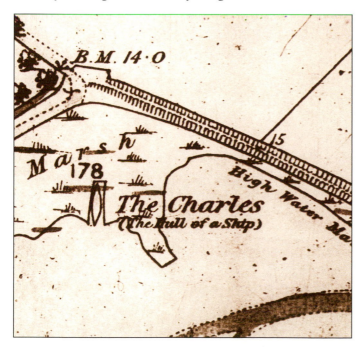

most parishes. This series is extremely useful for identifying field boundaries, but it is necessary to consult the accompanying notes (if they survive) that list boundary and ownership details about the town, parish or tithing.

There are a number of scales to be aware of in Ordnance Survey maps. By 1863 it had been decided to complete the 1-inch survey started in 1801, but also to map the whole country at 6 and 25 inches to the mile. A new series was started in 1932, which became known as the Pathfinder series (scale 1:25,000). This series has the most appropriate scale and clarity for fieldwork. For detail, however, nothing can beat the first edition of 25-inch maps. These maps are among the finest ever engraved. The detail is on occasion staggering; hedges, with tree species marked, parish and county boundaries delineated are just some of the rich topographic data available on these superb maps.

It is possible to photocopy the maps held for your area at the local Record Office or library, but beware of infringing copyright. Otherwise, Ordnance Survey maps can be ordered from an approved supplier. There are, however, a number of additional services which are provided by the OS:

Historic mapping: All County Series and National Grid sheets are available, produced from an archive dating to the early nineteenth century. These monochrome copies are available at a variety of scales and paper sizes.

Fig 16 The 1867 25-inch scale Ordnance Survey map of Milton Creek in Kent. Of particular interest is the nautical archaeology shown — the wreck of the Charles and associated quays and wharfs.

Aerial photography: Aerial maps are available from Getmapping, which provides the most comprehensive and detailed aerial photography survey of the UK at 1:1,250, and from Ordnance Survey aerial photography, which also offers vertical aerial photography as negatives, contact prints or on digital software.

Landplan: This is the new breed of mapping. For the first time, the Ordnance Survey has combined map and database information to produce user-friendly digital maps of great definition and accuracy. Landplans can be centred on any specific site and are available at 1:10,000 or 1:5,000 scales.

Superplan: These maps provide the most flexible form of customised graphic mapping of Britain. Site-centred mapping is available for the whole of Britain and can be produced at any scale from 1:100 to 1:5,000. Superplan data is supplied as electronic files by email, floppy disk or CD. The unique layering system within the data allows maps to be designed to your own specification and printed out at any given scale you choose.

Siteplan: These maps are designed for domestic planning applications but are extremely useful for archaeological sites. Three scales are available, 1:500 scale (giving 80m x 80m of ground coverage), 1:1,250 scale (giving 200m x 200m of ground coverage) and 1:2,500 scale (giving 400m x 400m of ground cover). Siteplan is also available by email in tiff format that can be opened with most Microsoft Word packages.

Fig 17 OS Superplan (right) can be supplied to any scale you so wish whilst OS Siteplan (above) are designed to accompany domestic planning applications.

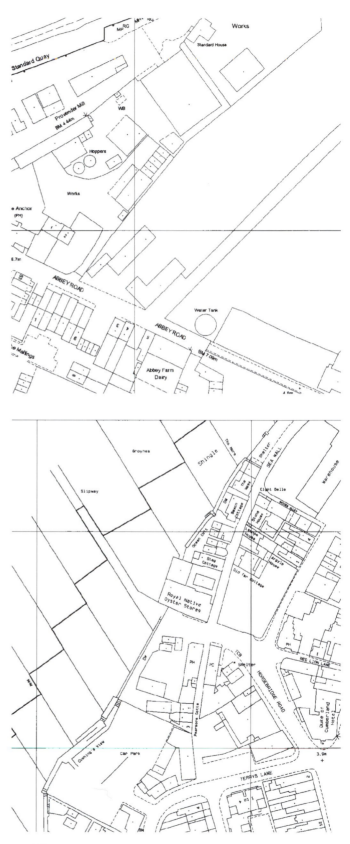

Place names

As Margaret Gelling says: 'Place names are important to the archaeologist and historian. Quite apart from the inherent interest of the original meaning of a place name, the fact that in England there are six successive layers of language reflected in the stock of place names means that they provide vital evidence' (Gelling, Signposts to the Past, 1997).

Names should not be taken at their face value, but need to be carefully interpreted after scrutiny of the earliest spelling, usually in the Domesday Book or earlier Anglo-Saxon charters. Modern names can have different origins. For instance, the name Broughton can mean 'brook farmstead', 'hill farmstead', or 'fortified farmstead' whilst different modern spellings can have identical origins. Thus Chiswick and Keswick were both originally 'cheese farm'.

It is an area of research for the specialist, and as Margaret Gelling says: 'Because place-name etymology abounds with snags of this kind, it is not possible to invite general participation in the process of suggesting etymologies. The rules have been objectively established; they are not arbitrary but they are intricate, and few non-specialists master them well enough to be on safe ground in this branch of the study'. The literature available for study is vast. The English Place-Name Society produces county volumes. Margaret Gelling has written many books on the subject, as has K. Cameron, E. Ekwall and F. M. Stenton. For Kent the standard work is by Wallenberg 'Place Names in Kent'.

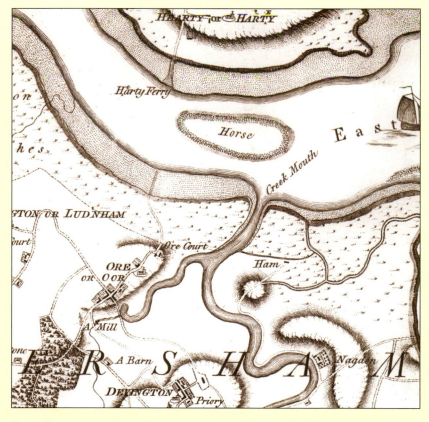

Fig 18 This early map of Faversham dates from the eighteenth century. The name Faversham is unique; it means 'the town of the Roman metal smiths' whilst 'Ham' can mean an early Anglo-Saxon farm. 'Ore' to the west of the creek is an unusual Jutish name which can mean 'shore', 'hill-slope' or 'boundary', all of which are applicable here. To the north is 'Haerty' or 'Heorot', as written in the saga Beowulf whilst 'Nagden' is thought to be Icelandic and means a burial mound with a stone marker.

CHAPTER TWO: AERIAL SURVEY FOR ARCHAEOLOGISTS

'If you are studying the development of the landscape in an area, almost any air photograph is likely to contain a useful piece of information'
(Interpreting the Landscape from the Air, Mick Aston, 2002).

Aerial photography is one of the most important remote sensing tools available to archaeologists. Other remote sensing devices are satellite imagery and geophysics. All of this information can be combined and processed through computers, and the methodology is known as Geographic Information Systems (GIS).

The development of aerial photography goes hand-in-hand with the development of the aeroplane and camera. A 1907 photograph taken on a plate camera in a balloon floating above Stonehenge (Fig 19) is one of our earliest aerial photographs, whilst in 2003 satellite imagery of the Iraq deserts revealed to American archaeologists hundreds of miles of buried roads from the earliest empires of that region. An early pioneer in aerial photography was O.G.S. Crawford. Funded by the marmalade millionaire, Alexander Keiller, Crawford photographed, from the air, archaeological sites in central southern England. The results were published in the classic book, *Wessex from the Air* (Crawford and Keiller, 1928).

Crawford collected aerial photographs from as many sources as possible, but mainly from the RAF. Working prior to the massive destruction by the ploughing up of archaeological features in the landscape in the Second World War and after, the images revealed some remarkable features. Much of Crawford's collection can still be seen in the NMRC in Swindon. During the Second World War there were huge advances in

technology. Aerial reconnaissance, carried out by specialist units of air forces, benefited from these advances and produced first-class aerial photographs. A number of archaeologists were involved in aerial photograph interpretation, and

Fig 19 One of the earliest oblique aerial photograph taken in 1907 on a plate camera from an army hydrogen balloon floating above Stonehenge in Wiltshire.

after the war an aerial photographic unit was founded by Keith St Joseph, which in 1949 became the Cambridge University Committee for Air Photography (now the Unit for Landscape Modelling). Its contribution over the last 60 years has been invaluable, with hundreds of sites located all over Britain. The Cambridge

Collection is available for study and is important because an aerial photograph taken, say, 30 years ago will show features in the landscape that may have now been removed by modern farming. In 1967 The Royal Commission on the Historical Monuments of England (RCHME)

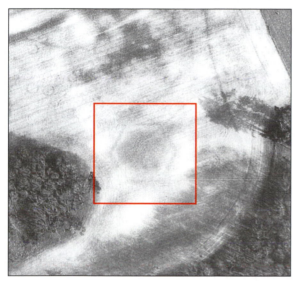

Fig 20 A 1946 vertical aerial photograph showing a hexagon-shaped feature near Canterbury. This feature was thought to date from the Second World War, but examination by the Kent Archaeological Field School revealed an early Roman cremation site surrounded by a Anglo-Saxon cemetery which overlaid an Iron Age settlement.

organised a national aerial reconnaissance programme which entailed the collection of existing aerial photographs, the acquisition of the RAF's historic collection of photographs, especially the 1946-8 series. The success of this policy can be seen in the growth of the collection from a few thousand to over 400,000 oblique and 2.4 million vertical aerial photographs all held at the NMR centre at Swindon.

How to use aerial photographs

Aerial photographs are merely raw data; they are a means to an end. The photograph needs to be examined so that the terrain can be interpreted and archaeological traces from features such as

Roman roads, lost settlements, forts, villas, canals and old river beds located.

Aerial photographs are of two main types; the oblique and the vertical. Each has its advantages and drawbacks.

Oblique aerial photographs, taken at an angle to reveal contours and shadows, are best for discovering sites, whilst vertical photographs are more useful for mapping. However, it is possible, using appropriate computer software programmes and at least four known points on the ground, to map an area quite accurately from an oblique aerial photograph.

Vertical photographs can be overlapped to give a three-dimensional effect through stereoscopic viewing lenses. Oblique photographs taken at low altitude are the most important means of discovering sites from the air because they provide perspective and a clearer view than vertical photographs. Also obliques are usually taken specifically for the purpose, whereas verticals are taken for general or planning purposes.

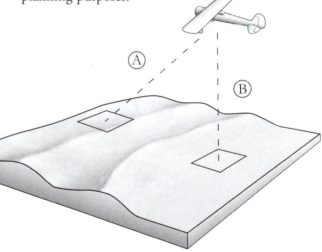

Fig 21 Photographs taken from an aircraft are usually of two types: a vertical photograph (B) taken directly below the aircraft is usually used for mapping purposes, whilst photographs taken at an angle are oblique photographs (A) and are usually taken of points of interest on the ground.

Fig 22 The modern oblique aerial photograph shows to good advantage the World Heritage Site of Stonehenge in Wiltshire.

Fig 23 The vertical aerial photograph of a motte and bailey castle taken by English Heritage in 1997 shows that the motte has been terraced to allow spiral access to the summit as part of a landscaped garden in the post-medieval period.
The site, Maiden Bower in North Yorkshire was built in about AD1071 and re-fortified in 1174. This is a good example of the kind of information which aerial photography can record when the conditions are right.

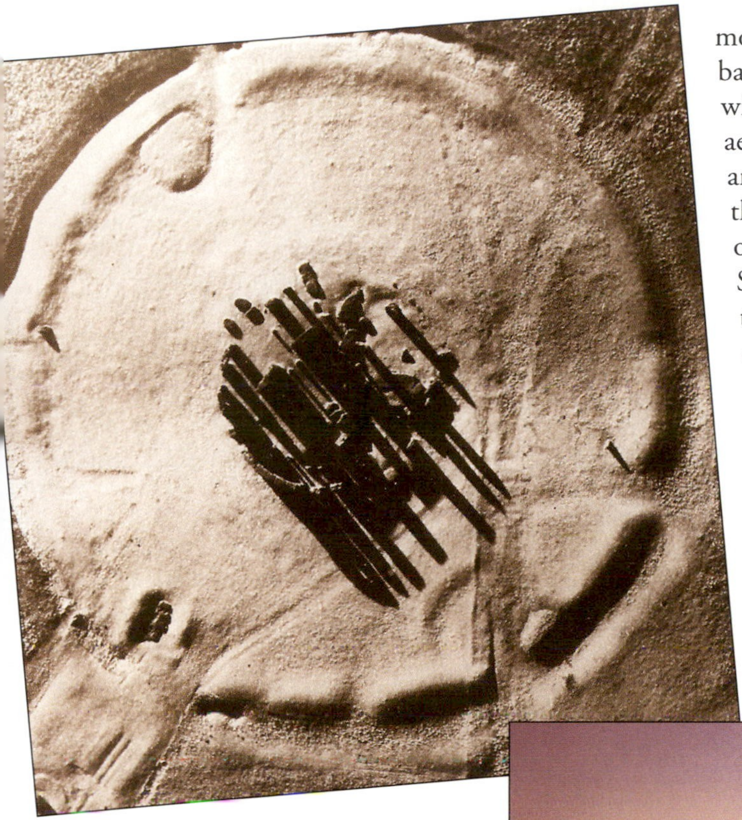

more or less at right angles to the sun's rays. If a bank or ditch runs parallel to the rays of light it will be difficult to see. It is essential to take aerial photographs at different times of the day and different times of the year to capture all of the site features to be seen, and a slight dusting of snow will also enhance features on the site. Shadow sites can also be seen and surveyed on the ground, but crop and soil marks can generally only be seen from the air.

Crop mark sites are some of the best indicators of buried features on a site. The variation in height of the crop, colour and vigour of growth can help find features beneath the surface. Where the soil is damp, as in a buried ditch or pit, the vegetation will be taller, greener and more dense. This is a positive crop mark. But over a buried

Fig 24 Vertical aerial photograph of a shadow site. Stonehenge photographed (above) early on a winter morning. The banks are brightly lit whilst the surrounding ditches are in shadow. Unfortunately the detail around the stones is lost because of the deep shadows.
A classic photographic (right) of an iconic site - Stonehenge at dawn.

There are three main visible archaeological features to be identified from aerial photography: shadow sites, crop mark and soil mark sites. Shadow sites are usually the most visible archaeological features to be seen in the landscape. Any site with lumps and bumps like banks or ditches has the potential to show shadows. In the raking light of low sun, early or late in the day, the site can spring to life in fascinating detail. Shadows will only be cast

building the soil above the walls will be thinner, drier, and the vegetation will be sparser and not so lush. This is a negative crop mark.

The greener, denser vegetation appears darker from the air and dark, almost black on existing black and white aerial photographs. Visibility of crop marks will change throughout the growing season, and indeed on a day-to-day basis. Different crops will react differently to soil

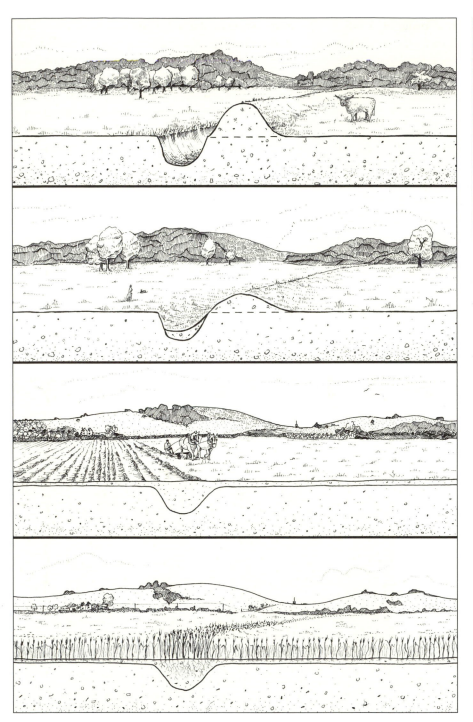

Fig 26 Part of the double ditch of the Roman frontier, the very edge of Empire somewhere in Germany. It is easily visible from the air as a crop mark.

Fig 25 The drawing above shows how an Iron Age ditch, forgotten and filled in by time and weather, becomes a buried archaeological feature revealed by the crops growing taller and greener.
Such variations in colour and height may not be obvious from the ground but are often clearly visible from the air.

conditions, and in the years of drought, 1946, 1947, 1976 and 1984, hundreds of new sites were identified. It is worth noting that grass has to be really parched before any buried features become apparent.

The most useful plants to produce crop marks are wheat, barley, peas, sugar beet, and maize. If a site is subject to crop rotation it will be most useful to take aerial photographs over a number of years. For the corn crops — wheat, barley, oats — it is worthwhile to keep an eye on the field, and as the crop turns from green to yellow to photograph it from the air. This will be the optimum time to discover crop marks.

Soil marks are usually at their best in ploughed fields. Every feature on an archaeological site is likely to be made out of different soils. Colour

and texture of the soil is the key indicator to the understanding of any archaeological site. Ditches may be in-filled with a dark silty soil; robbed wall foundations may show as streaks of grey lime mortar; ploughed-out barrows may show as a dark circle enclosing streaked re-deposited natural soil. Differences in moisture can reveal hidden ditches or even the walls of a buried building. After rain, the buried building's walls will retain moisture longer than the surrounding soil and leave a damp mark. Conversely, after frost, the cold walls of a buried building will retain the frost over the buried walls longer than will the surrounding soil (Fig. 29). These soil mark patterns may be extremely clear on a dry day or very blurred because of long-term ploughing of the site. Either way, they are a good indicator of the survival of the buried features as seen from the air.

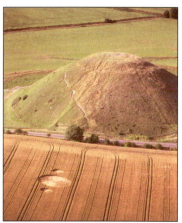

Fig 27 Aerial photograph of Neolithic and Bronze Age sites visible in the drought of 1995 (left). The central feature is called Church Henge after the Norman church located inside it. The surrounding earthworks have been protected from damage by the plough, a common source of damage. Silbury Hill (above) is close to collapse due to illegal digging.

Fig 28 These typical oblique aerial photographs reveal, in minute detail, the layout of an enormous courtyard Roman villa at Warfusee-Abancourt (Nord) and (right) at Grivesnes in the Somme area of France.
Both of the oblique pictures were taken early on a frosty morning by Roger Agache, an amateur archaeologist who is a dentist by profession.

Fig 29 Crop marks (right) show the buried foundations of Roman rectangular buildings outside of a Roman fort at Hungen-Inheiden in Germany.
The oblique air photograph is part of an area survey, conducted by the State Archaeological Service, (SAS) with stunning results.

How to take aerial photographs

Archaeological sites which may be visible as crop marks or soil marks need to be photographed from the air. The photographs taken are the most tangible record of what has been seen, but aerial reconnaissance is a type of archaeological survey and needs to be plotted on to an OS map. The position of the sun and the time of day need to be taken into consideration. The sites to be looked at must be given a site number and this site number can be marked on the canister containing the exposed film to enable identification at a later date. Nothing is more frustrating than having an aerial photograph of a new site and not knowing exactly where it is. If you photograph archaeological sites in a logical sequence the strips of film will enable you to identify forgotten monuments.

If your aircraft is equipped with the Global Positioning System (GPS) then a recording of the route of the flight can be printed out on an OS map. Another advantage of GPS is that any number of flights over a site can be recorded over a period of years.

Equipment

The first requirement is a high-wing aircraft; this

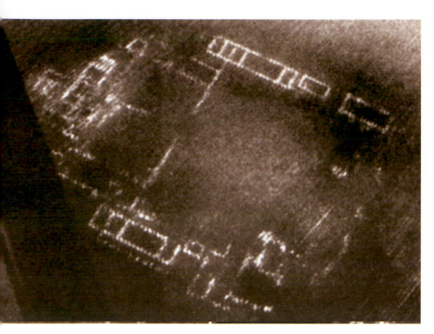

pay extra for the CD digital disk. You may not need it now, but digital photographs are the way forward both for viewing and archiving. It is also possible to use infra-red film, and the results can be stunning. The advantage of infra-red film is that it cuts out the blue light so the image can be much brighter and clearer.

Vegetation has a wide range of colours, but when viewed in infrared small changes of colour in crop growth can be seen much more clearly. The viewer has to remember that the colours are totally unreal and alien, with soil showing green and vegetation in varying intensities of red.

Maps

The OS 1:50,000 maps are ideal for in-flight navigation, but for mapping and interpretation a 1:10,000 map is best for aerial photograph interpretation. Each map should be marked up with the route to be flown and the sites to be recorded. Notes should be written up during the flight describing the route, and what was seen, what film and frame numbers were used and tied into a location with a six-figure OS grid reference.

Global Positioning Systems

GPS is used by many professional aerial surveyors and can replace much of the manual note taking and recording, but beware: if the GPS is not recording and you have decided not to take notes, then most of the flight data will be lost.

The weather

The best days for photography are those with still, clear air and little haze. For shadow sites, early morning and late afternoon in winter are best. This time of year has the added bonus that vegetation is at its minimum so earthworks usually hidden in long grass, shrubs and trees are visible. Dry summers are good for crop mark

means the wing is over the cockpit enabling an uninterrupted view below.

Aircraft in this category include the Cessna 150, 152 and 172. The window opens out and up and the photographer can literally lean out of the window to take photographs of the ground. Aircraft can be hired for about £170 an hour (2006), but it is also possible to join a local aero club and persuade a friendly pilot to take you up. Remember that Civil Aviation rules must be adhered to.

The camera

Any good 35mm camera with a standard 50mm 1.4f lens may be used. For better results a zoom lens will help enormously to focus on areas of interest on the ground. It is worth remembering that auto-focus cameras occasionally have difficulty focusing on the ground and may not work. If your camera starts misbehaving in this way, set the camera to infinity and put it on to manual mode.

Film

With digital cameras, of course, film is not required; otherwise colour print film from Kodak or slide film from Fuji are more than sufficient. With colour print film, order the 'large size' prints at the time of developing and formation, and dry autumns, after ploughing, for soil marks. Soil marks are at their clearest immediately after ploughing. Every time it rains the soil marks can diminish in clarity. Occasionally cold mornings will produce a frost which will melt more slowly on buried stone walls than on the surrounding soil.

A basic understanding of the types of sites likely to be encountered is essential. An understanding of the local geology is also necessary. Some geological features can be mis-identified as archaeological features. Each period of prehistory and history has left its own imprint on the landscape, sometimes recognisable as crop, soil or shadow sites.

Aerial photography cannot give, for a variety of reasons, total coverage of the landscape, but, just as in field-walking, constant and continuous survey will reveal new sites and add to our understanding of existing sites. Aerial survey is a means of discovering and recording sites, landscapes and buildings. It is also important as a first preparatory stage for local or regional field work. The archives of aerial photographs built up over the last 70 years and held in the national and local collections are invaluable and should be consulted prior to any initial work in the field. Whilst interpretation can take place in the air, intensive interpretation should take place more on the ground.

Fig 30 An oblique air photograph of the deserted shrunken medieval village at Goxhill, Humberside. Note the medieval ridge and furrow ploughed field at the top of the picture, the hollow ways and deserted building platforms. The features have survived because the area was used for pasture and never ploughed. Once ploughed all this would have disappeared.

Aerial photographs — what do they mean?
The two types of aerial photographs, vertical, or overhead, and oblique, or angled, can give away the secrets of the buried landscape in a spectacular manner. Ancient buildings, boundary walls and ditches, Roman forts and medieval villages will leave their mark on the landscape by their presence under the surface of the land. This alters the depth and consistency of the soil which in turn alters the growing pattern of the vegetation.

The effect on vegetation will change throughout the year and this is why it is necessary to photograph a site from the air at different times throughout the year. Plant growth will enhance the image of buried remains and some plants provide better contrast than others. Cereal grains will grow better over buried ditches which retain more moisture than the thin soil over buried walls or buildings. Cereals grow faster over buried ditches and rubbish pits, and there is usually a good colour difference to photograph. By contrast a field recently ploughed and harrowed will show soil marks where buried archaeological features have been disturbed and smeared across the contrasting soil (see below right).

False-colour infra-red aerial photography (below left) can be used with stunning effect, as this photograph of a Roman religious sanctuary at Saint-Usage in France shows.

CHAPTER THREE: GROUND SURVEY

'The interpretation of artefact scatters on their own is a hazardous business and …, though field walking is a powerful tool, its results need to be integrated with the results of other survey techniques, and excavation, to realise their full potential'
(Unravelling the Landscape, Mark Bowden, 1999).

Mark Bowden writes that the 'objectives of field walking are the location and characterisation of past human activity in the landscape. The aim is not to recover every artefact from the surface of the field but to collect a representative sample in a consistent manner, in order to map patterns which may reflect past activity.' There is an on-going debate about whether this representative sample should be returned to its exact location in the field after recording or kept for archiving.

There are a variety of ways of organising field walking, and these will depend on the aims of the survey and the resources available. Field walking has to be focused and used to answer questions about previous land use or human activity. In some cases it can follow the scrutiny of aerial photographs; in other cases the aim should be to locate and sample archaeological sites or enhance our knowledge of known archaeological areas.

The research design should indicate what sort of collection policy is to be undertaken. Is it to be an intensive collection, which will cover the complete area that has been laid out with a grid, or should it be more extensive, which will involve a sampling strategy over the entire area of landscape to be covered? For parish or regional surveys field walking in a random pattern in ploughed fields is a good way to start. At this stage no artefact collection should take place but notes should be made on a recording form (Fig 32) of what type of artefact is being

encountered. If artefacts need to be removed for specialist analysis then the exact spot should be marked on the recording form.

Hand-held navigational GPS is an ideal way to record the approximate position (to 10 metres) of the find. Recent tests by Portable Antiquities officers indicate that an eight-figure national grid reference (NGR) can be obtained from

Fig 31 Artefact collection from the ploughzone — whether by eye and hand or metal detecting — needs to be methodical and recorded. This coin hoard was found by a metal detectorist in Bedfordshire.

basic machines. All fields need to have an area or field code number followed by the find number and year.

For more focused field walking, the field is divided by parallel lines, usually 25 metres apart, or by a grid composed of squares, usually of 25- or 10-metre squares. To see how to lay out a grid turn to Fig 35. It is preferable to use the OS National Grid as a survey framework, and then each individual survey area can have its own unique OS reference number. If field walking is undertaken over what is obviously an archaeological site, whether a Roman building, or scatters of worked flint, then it is more appropriate to subdivide the grid into 10- or 5-metre squares. For field walking by line, each line is divided into segments for recording purposes. Usually the lengths are equal to the spacing between the lines, so if the lines are laid out at a distance of 25 metres apart, then a new bag for finds is started at the beginning of every 25-metre length.

All artefacts are bagged in a clear plastic bag, which has to be clearly marked on the outside with permanent ink specifying the site code, the year and month of collection and the line or grid number. If possible, put a waterproof tag with the same information inside the bag; this can then accompany the artefacts through the sorting and washing stages. The collected material is sorted into categories, recorded and probably returned to its original position on the field. For more intensive surveys the grid system is more useful. The size of the

grid will be influenced by how detailed the survey needs to be. Usually the squares are 10 metres, but 5 metres may be more appropriate. One of the benefits of the grid system is that artefacts can be seen more clearly on a random search, given the way light reflects on some artefacts. Each square has its own unique number or letter (Fig 33) and collection is usually done by one or more archaeologists collecting within the squares for a set time. On larger squares it is usual for the archaeologists to line up on one side of each square and walk across the square in a moving line picking up all the artefacts they can see and then returning across the same square from another direction.

With the growing interest in landscape archaeology and regional surveys in the 1970s and 80s, the big question was: what did it all mean? It was quickly recognised that the results of a field walking survey had to be used with caution. The scatter of artefacts across a field is as likely to be the result of manuring of arable fields by farming communities as from the surfacing of disturbed material from a buried archaeological site. To be able to understand the results of field walking, the information should be shown as a series of diagrams which will indicate the density of different types of artefacts in any given field. It is possible to produce this information this by the use of proportional circles in the case of a gridded field or differing thicknesses of line for

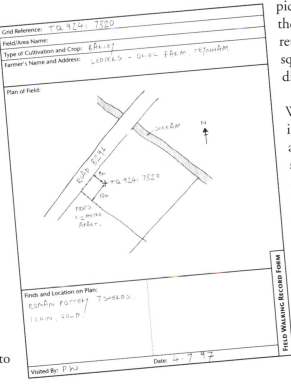

Fig 32 A typical field recording form from the Swale Archaeological Survey in Kent.

fields that have been line-walked (Fig 34).

Field walking is best carried out in winter. The more recent rain, frost and weathering ploughed fields have had the better. However, farming is now so intensive in some areas that the ploughed fields are not left to weather, but are ploughed, harrowed and planted within a few days. On these fields, field walking should take place after the crops have begun to show. Bright or low-angled sunlight makes it difficult to recognise surface artefacts. The best results are obtained in overcast conditions. Similarly, many smaller artefacts show up better in light rain, or after heavy rain has washed them clean.

It is possible to field walk an area that has not been ploughed. In landscapes planted with orchards the method to use is to field walk the orchard noting the artefacts lying on the surface around the trees. These are a direct result of the farmer digging a hole to plant the tree and in so doing disturbing a buried archaeological site.

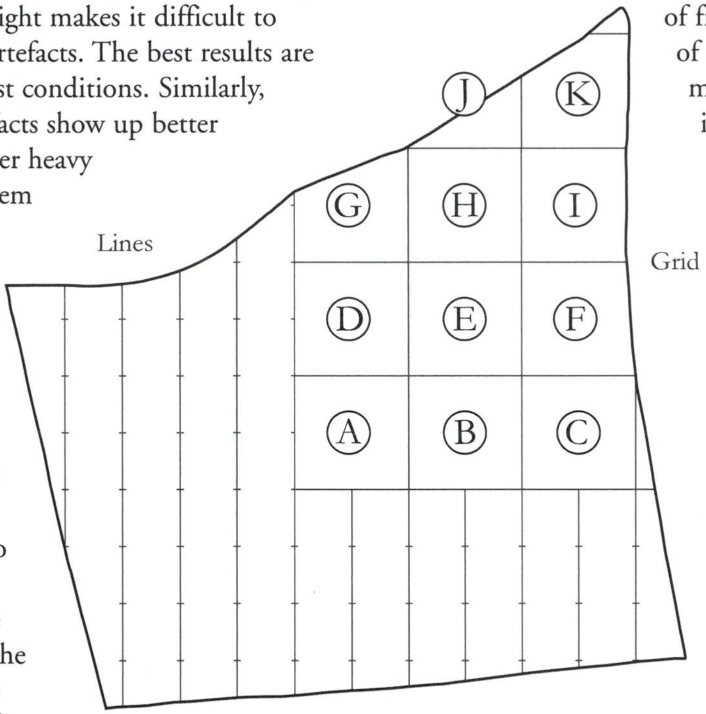

Lines — Grid

Fig 33 The method of field walking by line and grid shown at Field 4016 near Shapwick, by Mick Aston.

Metal detecting survey

Every year in England and Wales hundreds of thousands of archaeological objects are discovered by people using metal-detectors. These objects offer an important and irreplaceable source for understanding our past. The government is keen to encourage the voluntary recording of all archaeological finds and is, with the help of the Heritage Lottery Fund, funding the Portable Antiquities Scheme

(www.finds.org.uk) to proactively record archaeological finds discovered by the public across the whole of England and Wales for public benefit.

Detector finds help archaeologists and academic researchers to understand the historic environment, distribution patterns and artefact typology and help preserve ancient remains. Recording of finds is an essential part of modern detecting. To make useful finds records it is essential to have:

1. A hand held GPS (Global Positioning System) device and a good map, such as the OS Explorer series (orange cover). Of course the ability to read a map and take National Grid References (NGR) is essential!

Most of the finds discovered by metal-detectors will be post-1700. If you find earlier material it is necessary to record where the object was found (its find spot) using a GPS device and/or map. Individually bag the finds and record the find spot on the finds bag. If in doubt of the age of an artefact presume it is pre-1700 and record the find spot.

2. Finds recording forms: Record the find spot and details of the find (description, measurements and weight etc.) on a finds recording form. Take the form and artefact to your local Finds Liaison Officer, so it can be recorded on the national finds database – www.finds database.org.uk.

3. Field assemblage forms: Most metal-detectorists work in the same fields, and visit them time and time again. Field assemblage forms will help detectorists to get a feel for the archaeological potential of a given field over a period of time.

When detecting, put all your post-1700 finds into one bag, label it with the field reference number and complete a field assemblage form listing all finds (including pre-1700 finds). If your field is very big it will be necessary to draw a map on the back of the field assemblage form and divide the field into two, three or four parts (zones). Remember to bag finds from the different zones of the field into different clear plastic bags and number each bag with the appropriate field reference number or letter. List all your finds on the field assemblage form, giving a brief description and details of the metallic composition of the finds.

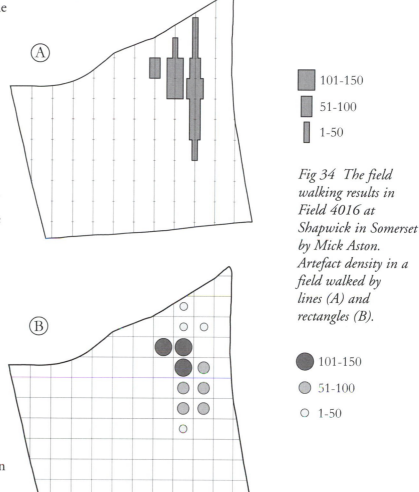

▮	101-150
▮	51-100
▮	1-50

Fig 34 The field walking results in Field 4016 at Shapwick in Somerset by Mick Aston. Artefact density in a field walked by lines (A) and rectangles (B).

●	101-150
●	51-100
○	1-50

Metal-detectorists are responsible for the vast majority of the metal finds recovered in Britain today and are probably the most active of field walkers. Recent studies show that over 90% of metal-detected finds are recovered from cultivated land where they are vulnerable to plough damage and natural corrosion processes, therefore 'responsible' metal-detectorists — those who report their finds and have them recorded — have an important part to play in the archaeological process.

It is therefore essential that access to finds recording by individual detectorists is promoted, if detectorists are to be better integrated into the archaeological process. However, it must be understood that any finds lifted from an archaeological context are of limited value to anybody who wants to understand the past.

Metal-detectors are increasingly utilised during archaeological investigations. In these circumstances it is standard practice for detectorists to relinquish rights to all finds (as archaeologists do), including treasure, found whilst detecting under archaeological supervision. It is therefore important that detectorists working on an archaeological site sign a 'Finds Agreement' to this effect.

Geophysical survey

Geophysical survey should be considered as one of the main techniques of site evaluation and interpretation. Its potential contribution to field survey must always be considered. The most important geophysical survey technique for amateur archaeologists is resistivity, followed closely by magnetometry. Geophysical specialists favour magnetometry above resistivity. The reasons are that it is the fastest method of rapidly covering very large areas to evaluate their archaeological content quickly. Magnetometry also responds to a wider range of archaeological features, so it is a very good general-purpose detection method.

However, if the purpose of the geophysical survey is specifically to target the continuation underground of the partially exposed walls of a monastic or castle site then resistivity would be the first choice, but for general purpose site exploration magnetometry would be the preferred method. Other techniques that can be used are ground-penetrating radar, acoustic reflection, thermal sensing, dowsing and probing.

Resistivity works on the principle that soils which contain water conduct electricity more effectively than natural rocks like granite, ragstone and chalk. As you pass a small electrical current through the ground, these rocks will resist more than the damp soil. This pattern of variable resistivity can be measured and recorded with a purpose-built meter. Amateur groups usually use resistivity because the equipment is less costly than that for other systems and is simpler to operate and process after for non-geophysical specialists. The depth limit of resistivity is dependent upon the probe arrangement. In the twin-probe configuration, a 0.5-metre distance between probes will rarely give many readings on features below 0.75 metres. Greater distance between the probes will increase the depth penetration, although at the expense of the resolution of features. Features normally identified as low-resistance anomalies include ditches, large pits, gulleys and occasionally graves. This is because ditches and pits have a lower resistance than buried stone walls and floors, unless filled with stony material. High-resistance anomalies include metalled roads, stone or brick walls, made-up surfaces as in floors or courtyards and, occasionally, stone coffins or cists. If using a twin electrode probe machine on a frame, one reading is taken in each metre square with the fixed probe outside the square. The reading in each square can be recorded manually or by using a data logger.

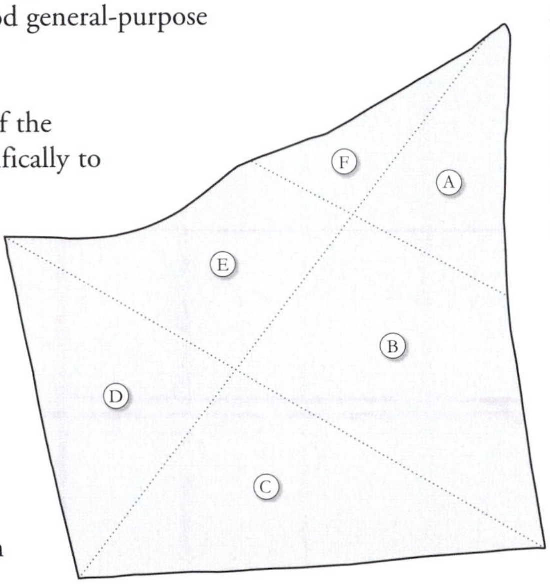

Fig 35 *The six zones (A to F) are not of an equal area or dimension. Large survey areas such as these suit detectorists, as the signals given and received by metal-detectors can be confused if detectorists work too close together. Division of the field is simplified by utilising the four corners of the field.*

To undertake a geophysical survey, a grid needs to be marked out and related to local permanent 'hard' features in the landscape so that it can be readily re-established for further work. Grids are the essential foundation of all archaeological survey and recording, and are explained in detail in Chapters five and six. Geophysical specialists will use a Trimble 4700/8000 series real-time kinematic GPS in stake-out mode to ensure the results can be repeated.

Fig 36 Print out of a geophysical survey of a large Roman villa (left) found by the KAFS field-walking at Newbury Farm near Sittingbourne in Kent. The building has a corridor, bath-house and three principal rooms plus additional buildings clustered around the main house Each cube of print-out is 1m square.

Fig 37 A colour enhanced geophysical survey of part of the Archbishops' Palace adjacent to the church at Teynham. The buried remains were found and investigated by the KAFS (below) and dated from the twelfth century; painted plaster walls, stained-glass windows and medieval floor tiles existed throughout most of the complex.

One GPS receiver is set up in stationary mode on a tripod over a base station point from where it continuously tracks the positions of the satellites. A second roving receiver that communicates by radio with the stationary receiver is used to set out the grid.

Fluxgate gradiometer

This is the most widely used geophysical instrument. Under ideal survey conditions features of archaeological interest can be recorded up to a depth of 1 metre. Its speed of use means large areas can be surveyed rapidly and the data recorded is reasonably easy to understand and interpret.

This technique records minor variations in the earth's magnetic field. Topsoil contains more magnetic oxides than subsoil, so soil silting into a ditch will locally affect the earth's local magnetic field.

The results of human activity, such as burning, and organic decomposition will probably accumulate in pits and ditches and so be detectable by gradiometer, which will measure this magnetic intensity on a meter. Needless to say, anything which is modern and magnetic, from a metal zip to a passing lorry, will affect readings and create problems. To undertake a survey a grid needs to be marked out.

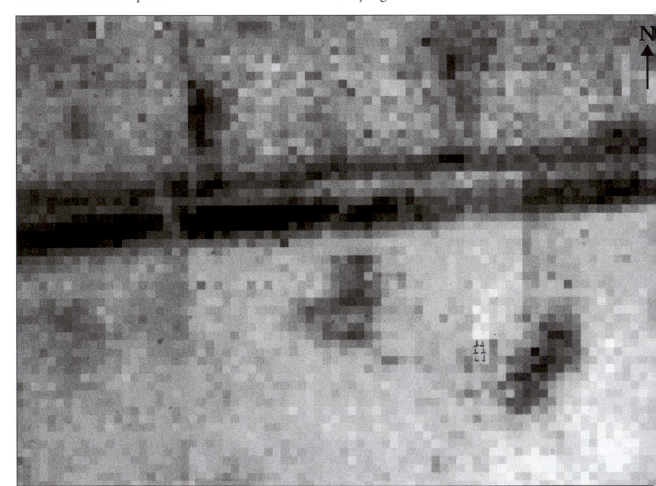

Fig 38 Resistivity survey of the Roman town of Durolevum found by the KAFS at Syndale Park near Faversham. The plot shows the buried Roman road (Watling Street) still surviving under the turf with the Roman town buildings either side of the road. Each square on the plot is one metre square.

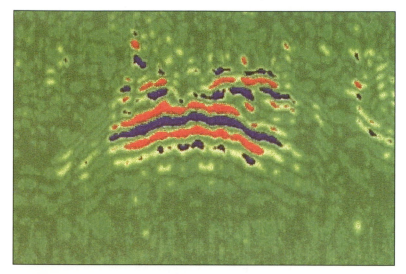

Under normal survey conditions a gradiometer survey will most probably locate ditches, pits, hearths, ovens, tile kilns, brick and tile remains, burnt mounds. Under very favourable conditions it will locate large postholes, gulleys and walls, and very strong magnetic features such as kilns can be detected at depths greater than one metre.

Ground penetrating radar (GPR)

The ultimate aim of geophysics is to produce a complete 3-D model of buried archaeological features that goes beyond the 2-D plans provided by traditional earth resistance and magnetic surveys. Ground penetrating radar operates by firing a series of short radar pulses into the ground and records both the timing and magnitude of returned signals. Due to the conical nature of the radar beam, the resulting mass of data is difficult to interpret without resorting to a powerful computer that will process the data numerically to form a series of 'time slices'. Each progressive slice represents reflections from features at an increasing depth, thereby creating a 3-D model of the buried target. Interesting

Fig 39 Time slices (top) using ground penetrating radar showing the various surfaces of a Roman road called Watling Street in Syndale Park, near Faversham. On excavation by the KAFS the construction of the road can be dated by artefacts to AD50, and at least seven phases of rebuilding can also be dated by artefacts and Roman coins. The route of the road is shown above (red line) on the aerial photograph. The road was abandoned in c.AD420, and household debris from the adjacent Roman town scattered across the road surface.

features can be enhanced by combining a series of such time slices in a computer animation. Indeed, this process may reveal an incredible wealth of detail in a buried structure. GPR requires a good contact between the ground surface and antenna. GPR is one of the few techniques suitable for sites covered in tarmac and concrete or even shallow water. The latest generation of GPR allows digital data to be collected every few centimetres along parallel paths and to a depth of several metres.

CHAPTER FOUR: ARCHAEOLOGICAL FIELD SURVEY

'Undertaking archaeological earthwork survey by graphical or plane table techniques is immensely rewarding. Seeing the plan grow and recognising patterns as they emerge…is a real thrill…. Finally, spending time on a site with a plane table or some tapes, in close physical contact with the ground, gives a depth of knowledge and understanding that cannot be gained in any other way'
(With Alidade and Tape, Mark Bowden, 2002).

It is likely that archaeological field survey began in 1649, when John Aubrey, a well-known 17th-century surveyor, saw the standing stones and earthworks at Avebury for the first time. His later survey in 1663 produced the first known accurate plan of Avebury. In the 18th-century, William Stukeley and John Horsley carried on in the tradition of Aubrey, and General William Roy established the discipline with his work on Roman sites in northern England and Scotland. There has been in recent years a renewed interest in archaeological field survey, much enhanced by the tremendous strides forward made by new survey techniques using GPS, aerial photography, field walking and geophysics survey.

Fig 40 The Rollright Stones in Oxfordshire. Recorded by William Stukeley on one of his topographic tours

Before starting a survey, walk around the landscape to see what features can be identified. You will need to try to interpret the features and how they relate to each other. It may be worthwhile researching comparable features in other areas. After your initial reconnoitre, work can start by consulting the records in order to find out what is known about the area under scrutiny. The information that can be gathered, as a desk-based exercise, would include:

1. Ordnance Survey (OS) maps including OS Surveyors' Drawings (British Library), OS historical maps, County Series, 1st and 2nd editions.
2. National Monuments Records (NMR).
3. Sites and Monuments Record (SMR).
4. English Heritage scheduled sites etc.
5. Published sources including County Archaeology Society records.
6. Pre-Ordnance Survey maps, estate maps, tithe maps, railway and canal surveys.
7. Aerial photographs (NMR, CUCAP).

Earthwork survey

Earthwork survey is usually tackled in three stages. They are reconnaissance, control survey and detail survey.

Reconnaissance

On the first reconnaissance visit, a walkover would take place to assess the archaeological potential of the area, the aims and purpose of the survey, access to the area, the number of people required and what type of survey equipment that will be needed. Ownership issues will need to be resolved, health and safety legislation addressed, and any other problems that may arise should be dealt with at this stage. Thorough preparation at this stage can save an awful lot of time later on.

Control survey

Before starting work it will be necessary to establish a control framework of fixed points on the ground and linked to each other by linear and angular measurements. You will find all survey consists of distance and angle measurements. The fixed points can be existing 'hard' features in the landscape — manhole covers, telegraph poles, corners of buildings — whilst other fixed points will be put in by the surveyor and could be pegs, survey buttons, etc. All these points are surveyed in and plotted on the site plan or control diagram.

On this drawing all other 'soft' archaeological detail is drawn. It is called 'soft' because the measured tops and bottoms of earthwork slopes are a matter for subjective judgement by the surveyor. Make sure the control points are not too close to archaeological features, otherwise the survey pencil lines on your drawing will obscure essential detail. Control points need to be established no more than 60m apart, otherwise tapes will have to be longer than 30m.

The selection of the correct scale is essential in recording any archaeological site. For landscape survey it is usual to survey at scales of 1:1000 or 1:500. English Heritage surveyors employ both scales but the larger scale, 1:500, is used if structural details of buildings are to be recorded.

For most landscape surveys of earthworks the smaller scale of 1:1000 is more appropriate.

Drawing in the field must be done on plastic drawing film using an appropriate pencil. It is a false economy to use tracing paper as it will cockle at the merest hint of damp. Also, it is good practice to prick through the film at the centre of the survey control points.

Electronic Distance Measurement (EDM) and Global Positioning Survey (GPS) are the two types of equipment usually used for establishing the main survey stations, but other manual methods can be used on any site that is not too large. Make sure most of the area to be surveyed is contained within the framework of these stations. If you do this, the survey measurements can be cross-checked and any errors corrected.

Mark the main survey stations with temporary or permanent pegs or markers. If there is the likelihood of livestock entering the field it is essential to have secure markers, otherwise they may be uprooted. Most survey supply companies sell survey markers with a built-in anchor device. The position of control stations should be carefully considered to ensure that all 'hard' detail and archaeological features can be easily seen and plotted from the control stations. There are three types of survey control that can be used.

Single control point

A single control point, usually located in the centre of the area to be surveyed, enables all the site to be surveyed from this single point. It is necessary to see the entire area to be surveyed from the single control point.

Base line traverse

Base line traverse uses two survey control points located at either end of a measured base line. It is essential to reference the measurements from each control point to each other and to the feature being surveyed.

Ring traverse

Ring traverse is used where three or more survey stations are established and measurements are taken from each station in turn. Again, it is essential to reference the measurements from each control point to each other and to the feature being surveyed. As measurements are taken around the ring any discrepancy will show on completion of the ring. If your measurements are correct you will be 'closing the traverse'; if not, you will have a 'misclosure' which will mean that your survey will have to be re-checked.

Detail survey

Once the control framework of fixed points has been established, the survey can move forward with the taking of earthwork measurements with much simpler equipment. The techniques that can be used are tape and offset with a plane table. During the process of measuring and drawing, an understanding of the earthworks, and their relationship to each other, will begin to form through discussion, and this procedure of observing the detail and measuring will help in the interpretation and understanding of the site.

Tape and offset

Tape and offset requires few people and very little equipment: 30m or 50m tape measures, ranging poles, optical square, pencil, scale ruler and set square. Lay out a tape measure between two control points, and lay out right-angled offsets where they are needed. Measure along these offsets to the tops and bottoms of slopes, changes of alignment of earthworks and any other features that need to be recorded. Offsets at the tops and bottoms of earthworks can then be joined with a solid line for the top of the slope and a pecked or dotted line for the bottom of the slope.

Hachures (see pages 44 and 71) will need to be drawn on site. It is good practice to write down on to your field sheet all measurements and plot these with your scale ruler before moving on to the next offset.

Remember that other measurements can be taken besides those along right-angle offsets. You can run on your straight base line and triangulate with other control points.

Intersections can be established with the optical square and measurements taped from them. It is essential that the control points are accurate; if they are then the resulting plan will be correct, but if they are not the drawing will be distorted.

Levelling

On a typical earthwork site it will be necessary to measure the profiles of banks and ditches so the extent of the features can be recorded on the field sheet. A simple method sometimes used involves setting up a horizontal line using ranging rods set vertically in the ground and attaching a line level, which is a small spirit level with hooks that can be hung on the line. Stretch a measuring tape along the line and with a hand tape measure down to the ground at regular intervals.

The results can be drawn up as vertical planning by offsets. For larger earthworks and slopes a pocket level can be used. Measure the observer's eye-height and, starting at the bottom of the slope, fix the spot on the slope that is being observed through the pocket level. The observer then walks up the slope to that spot and repeats the exercise. The height of the slope can then be calculated from the observer's eye-height multiplied by the number of observations taken. Make sure that when the observer reaches the top of the slope the extra height that can be gauged from a ranging rod is deducted from the total, as is the height of the observer.

Plane table survey

The plane table has been used by surveyors for at least the last 400 years. It consists of a tripod, a drawing board mounted horizontally on the tripod, an alidade (sight rule) and a spirit level to make sure the drawing board is exactly horizontal. To ensure that the correct ground position of the control point is on the table, a plumbing fork and plumb bob are used.

To set up the plane table there are three basic requirements:

1. It must be horizontal.
2. It must be correctly positioned over the control station.

Fig 41 Julian Richards explains to archaeologists the intricacies of landscape survey at Syndale Park.

3. It must be correctly orientated to the site. At the control point, set the table horizontal using the spirit level and make sure the whole set-up is fixed, level and firm and orientated to the site.

Place a sheet of 125-micron drawing film on the drawing board and attach it with masking tape. Make sure the plastic film is flat on the board and that the masking tape is stretched smooth so it does not impede the alidade when it is moved. With the plumbing fork and bob make sure the control point on the ground is pricked on the drawing film in the exact position vertically above the actual ground position of the control point.

There are two ways of using a plane table, by radiation and by intersection.

Radiation
Set up your plane table as explained and after marking your position on your plan you can use the alidade to draw out radiating lines to the points you want to record.

To use the alidade, place the alidade blade on the control point marker or ranging rod and, holding the alidade steady, draw a pencil line along the blade. This will give you a line radiating to the point you want to record. The distance from the table to the control point can then be measured on the ground and drawn on to the plan.

If you wish to record further detail it is possible to plot measurements by using tapes and an optical square to capture any detail at right angles to the drawn ray. Remember that all measurements by tape must be horizontal in all aspects of survey.

Intersection
The second method involves using a base line and is a type of triangulation. Set the table up at one end of the base line and mark the position of the control point on your drawing film. Plot in all the intersection lines in the manner explained and move the plane table to the other end of the base line and repeat the exercise, sighting on the same control points.

There are some key principles that must be remembered when undertaking a landscape survey with a plane table.
1. Do not lean on the drawing board. If you accidentally move the set-up from its original position then the drawing will not be accurate.
2. Always make checks on all of your measurements. Step back from your plan now and then and compare your drawing with the real thing in front of you.
3. Check the orientation of the board from time to time and at the end of drawing.
4. Draw lightly. Do not obscure the drawing with unnecessarily long or heavy radiation lines.
5. Always work from the whole site to the parts. This means planning in all the control points and 'hard' features before filling in the 'soft'

Steep-sided ditch Shallow ditch Gentle slope Natural slope

Examples of mound depiction

Fig 42 Hachure depictions of earthworks and associated features.

earthwork details.

Depiction

The artificial slopes of archaeological earthworks are usually shown by hachures (see above). These conventions are used in order to represent a three-dimensional earthwork on flat paper or film. For instance, slopes are shown by elongated delta-shaped lines which are drawn with the delta head at the top of the slope and the tail running down to the bottom of the slope, the size and shape of which are exactly related to the profile and gradient of the earthwork. The length of hachure represents the horizontal length of the slope and the spacing between the individual hachures indicates the steepness of that slope. The closer the spacing of the hachures the greater the gradient on the earthwork.

On a number of sites the natural slope of the ground is of interest to archaeologists and can reveal much about the positioning of

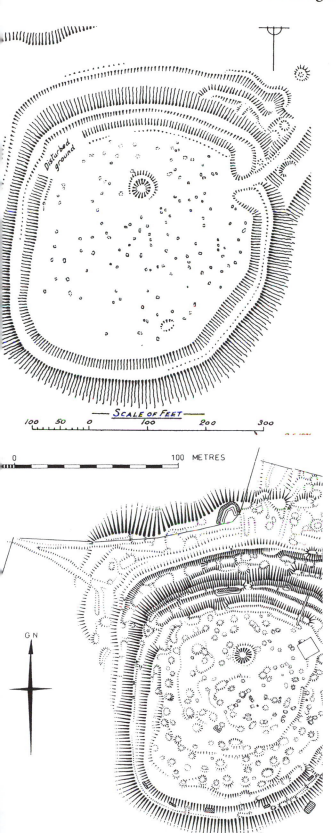

Scale of Feet
100 50 0 100 200 300

0 100 METRES

G N

archaeological earthworks. In most cases depicting the natural slopes with a different style of hachure is sufficient, but on some sites it may be necessary to record the contours of the topography at suitable vertical intervals. Such survey tasks are not to be undertaken lightly, as they can be one of the most tedious exercises in survey. Although a contour survey can be undertaken manually, it is more usual now to use GPS equipment and digital ground modelling software.

The field drawings that are produced by an archaeological landscape survey will show all of the control stations, the 'hard' and 'soft' detail and usually be covered in copious notes if a notebook has not been used. It is essential to make sure the field drawings are marked with the name of the site, any necessary reference number, a magnetic north arrow which is dated, because magnetic north changes by a few degrees each year, the scale used on the drawing, the date the survey was undertaken and the names of the people involved in the survey.

The field drawings will be used to create the archive drawing which is an accurate tracing of the field drawings, but the tops of the earthworks and the bottoms of slopes are replaced by hachures. Details of the original survey, including control points, can be left out and all annotation replaced by type.
The site location information is retained, but magnetic north is usually replaced by grid north. The plan should be accompanied by a written report that will have used material from the field notes and plans. It will include an understanding of the site including the chronological interpretation of the various earthworks, the general setting, and any future threats to the site.

Fig 43 An early plan of Mount Caburn, Sussex, an Iron Age hillfort and a more recent hachured survey by A. Oswald and D. McOmish of the RCHME (English Heritage).

Survey, excavation, recording and reconstruction

A classic example of utilising the various archaeological survey disciplines was in the discovery in 2004 by the Kent Archaeological Field School (KAFS) of an important Roman aisled building at Hog Brook near Deerton Street, Kent.

The buried remains of the building were discovered by field-walking. A metal detector survey was done under archaeological supervision and a programme of investigation carried out by students of the KAFS. The remains exposed and recorded enable us to say the building was aisled with 20 masonry piers holding up a substantial terracotta roof. Pottery and personal items found in situ on the sandy floor are Anglo-Saxon and date from the late 5th and early 6th centuries. Roman pottery found in the foundation trenches of this enormous stone building indicate the structure was built in the late first century AD as part of a large villa complex.

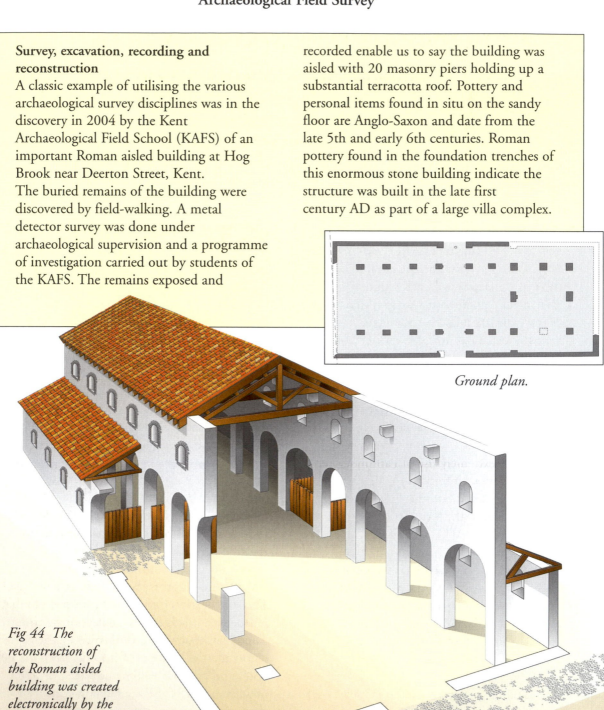

Ground plan.

Fig 44 The reconstruction of the Roman aisled building was created electronically by the artist using the excavation reports and referring to similar buildings found throughout the western Roman Empire.

CHAPTER FIVE: SITE EXCAVATION AND THE SITE GRID

'Archaeological surveying is a skill which many archaeology students and excavators believe, wrongly, to be beyond their comprehension'
(Surveying for Archaeologists, F. Bettes, 1992).

Accurate location of an archaeological site with reference to the Ordnance Survey (OS) national grid and datum is as important as the accurate location of archaeological data within a site. There is a good guide to taking grid-references on the OS website (www.ordnancesurvey.co.uk). The most useful maps for archaeologists are the Explorer Series, at a scale of 1:25,000. This scale means that 40 millimetres on the map corresponds to 1 kilometre on the ground. Ordnance Survey produces three types of map at this scale: the Explorer Series with an orange cover; Outdoor Leisure maps with a yellow cover; and the extremely useful Pathfinder Series with a green cover. Unfortunately the Pathfinder Series is being phased out, but it is worthwhile purchasing maps in the series whilst they are still available.

All of these maps, and indeed any modern Ordnance Survey map, are overprinted with a grid, the lines of which are spaced at 1-kilometre intervals. The numbers of each grid line are printed on the edges of the map, and always consist of two digits.

All Ordnance Survey maps are orientated to OS Grid north. The north-south vertically orientated grid lines are called easting, because the numbering increases to the right of the map, which of course is the east. The east-west horizontally orientated grid lines are called northing, because their numbers increase north-wards towards the top of the map. The grid lines on a map are part of the National Grid that

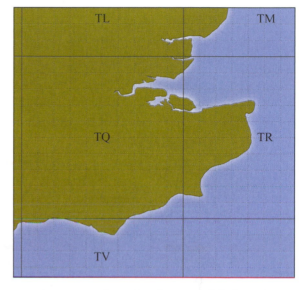

Fig 45 National Grid Reference. Alphabetical codes of the 100-kilometres squares covering south-east England.

divides all of Britain into 100-kilometre squares. Each 100-kilometre square has its own double letter code, which should always prefix the numerical code to follow. The first stage of locating a site is to establish which 100-kilometre grid square the site is in. The letter code of the 100-kilometre grid is printed on the green covers of the Pathfinder maps, or in the general information section adjacent to the key of symbols in the yellow Outdoor Leisure maps and the orange Explorer maps. The second stage is to locate the easting and northing grid lines which delimit the kilometre squares. It is important to remember that all grid references are taken from the bottom left or south-west corner of the map. From this corner, find the easting by reading the value of the vertical line nearest the site running up the map, and then work out the northing by reading the value of the nearest horizontal line running across the map.

If it sounds difficult or confusing look at the map below. St Luke's Church is located in the kilometre grid square 65 51. It is important to

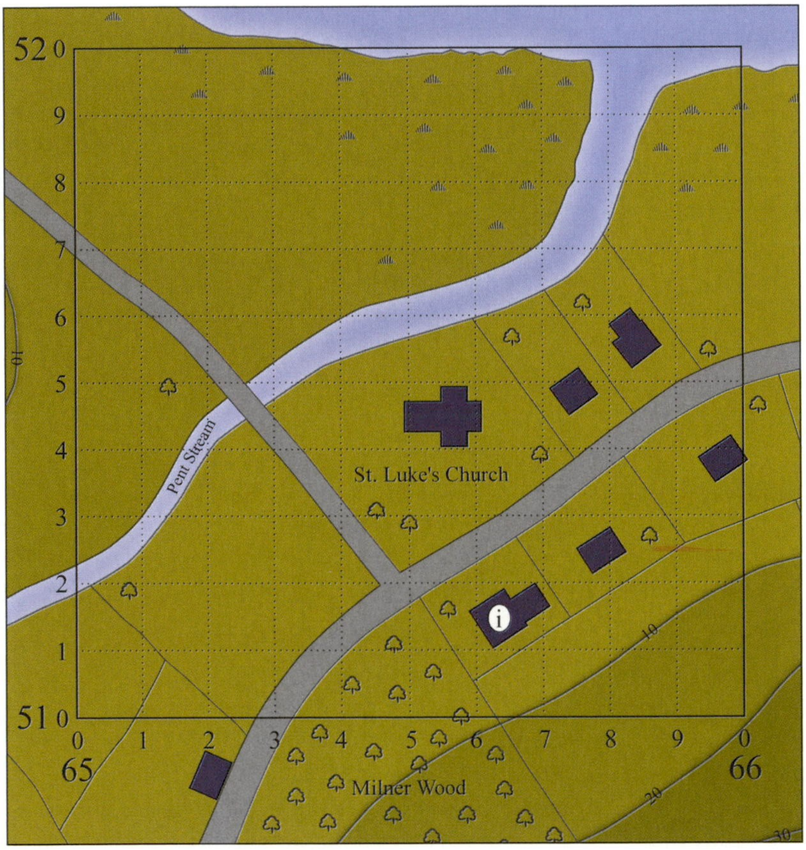

Fig 46 Six- and eight-figure grid references.

remember that the easting grid reference should always be given first. To give a more precise grid reference it is necessary to quote it to either six or eight figures. A six-figure grid reference is equivalent to a 100-metre square, whilst an eight-figure grid reference is equivalent to an area of 10 metres square. Each kilometre square is divided into ten further eastings and northings using the graduated scales printed on the edges

of the Ordnance Survey map. To obtain a six-figure grid reference read off the figures in exactly the same way as the four-figure grid reference was calculated, then count the number of units on the graduated scales. Look at the map in Fig 46: the six-figure grid reference for the tourist information centre close to St Luke's Church is 656 511.

To obtain a good fix it is best for the inexperienced to use a clear plastic ruler for sighting along. To obtain an eight-figure grid reference that will locate a site in a 10-metre square, it is necessary to subdivide the 100-metre square into a hundred smaller squares. Then read off the figure for the easting and the northing, but it will be necessary to use a scale ruler to calibrate the divisions. Again, look at the map; the eight-figure grid reference for the middle of the information centre near St Luke's Church is 6564 5115.

Site location

Any excavation or find made in a field needs to be located exactly to the National Grid. The procedure is simple and can be achieved with the minimum of survey equipment.

1. Draw and record the exact dimensions of the trench or area of find.
2. Select three reference points on the trench that can be recognised from the exact dimensions of the site drawing — usually three of the corners.
3. Always obtain a large-scale Ordnance Survey map of the area. On the map note at least three points of reference which are 'hard' detail, i.e. points of reference that are unlikely to move or

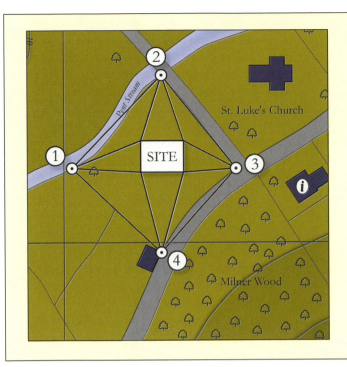

Known points

1. Edge of field boundary and stream.

2. Edge of bridge across stream.

3. Edge of roads.

4. Corner of building.

Fig 47 Fixing the position of a site grid by triangulation from known points.

deteriorate in the next few years.

4. From these points of reference measure on the ground (keeping the tape horizontal) the distance to the three chosen points of reference of the trench.

5. Set a pencil compass to the distance measured on a scale ruler to the same scale as your Ordnance Survey map (e.g. 1:50).

Draw an arc from each of the three points of reference measured on the ground and marked on the map, and where the arcs intersect will be the exact location and dimensions of the trench or area of find. If the scale drawing is 1:50 then 1.5m on the ground will be 15mm on the scale plan. If a number of scattered trenches needs to be surveyed into the National Grid it is possible to set up a control point or points on known Ordnance Survey features by using a site level, theodolite, plane table, or simply use a compass (but beware, a compass is the least accurate). On the large-scale Ordnance Survey map, use a protractor to plan in the degrees taken by the compass. However, do keep in mind that the north on Ordnance Survey maps is grid north

and not magnetic north as shown on the compass. If the intent is to plan in a compass bearing on to an OS map, add the appropriate deviation and date the drawing.

The site grid

The skeleton of any recording system is the site grid, which should cover the entire area of excavation. Most sites need only a 10-metre square grid, although on complex sites the use of a 5-metre square grid will be more beneficial. All plans of contexts are drawn by reference to the site grid, and drawn sections are also located by reference to the site grid. To set out a site grid first walk around the site and try to imagine any future excavation requirements. It is usual to orientate the site grid lines to true north but if there are suitable permanent features, like a concrete path or building, then orientate the site grid to these. The southern edge of the site grid is usually the site baseline and, just like Ordnance Survey maps, the south-west corner of the site grid is the point of origin for numbering the squares of the grid. It may be, on occasion, necessary to set the grid from another baseline and, on occasion, it is more reliable to set out the baseline across the centre of the site. This will ensure the grid is more accurate where accuracy is most needed.

To set out a baseline, stretch a tape tightly along the preferred line and put in marker pegs at intervals at whatever square measurement has been chosen, for instance at 5-metre or 10-metre intervals. The site grid exists only in the horizontal plan so it is important to ensure the tape is horizontal by attaching to it a line level. Use a plumb bob to ascertain the accurate location of a point on the grid. Measure

distances on the grid to the nearest 1cm. A variety of marker pegs is available to set out the grid. Traditionally a wooden peg was driven in and a nail knocked into the top of the peg, which enabled small adjustments to be made to the measured distance. It is now more usual to use steel rods which can be driven into the ground and capped with a plastic 'mushroom' or a brightly painted wooden block marked with the site grid co-ordinates.

To measure triangulated distances inside the grid, the end of the tape can be slipped on to the rod once the wooden or plastic cap has been removed. The main grid line has now been set out and it is necessary to set out the second main grid line at right angles to the first.

Fig 48 Site grid in operation. Students from the KAFS are practising the technique of trowelling within a site grid divided into 1-metre transections.

Site Excavation and the Site Grid

If the grid is being set out with a theodolite or optical site level, the grid baseline will have been set and it will only be necessary to turn 90 degrees on the theodolite scale to establish the second main grid line, which will be at right angles to the first line. If you do not have a theodolite or EDM the right-angle will have to be set off accurately using tapes and wooden or metal marker pegs.

One of the easiest ways to set off a right-angle is to remember that the hypotenuse or diagonal of a 5-metre square is 7.07 metres and of a 10-metre square 14.14 metres. Place a tape on one of the marker pegs on the main 5 metre grid line (the baseline), put another tape on the next marker peg but one, draw out both tapes to 7.07 metres, for a 5-metre square, and where they intersect place another marker peg. The intersection point is on a line that is at right angles to the main grid line from the marker peg located between the two marker pegs that were utilised for the diagonal measurements. The right-angle grid line is now established.

Extend the line by tape and repeat the exercise. All of the main grid line intersection points can now be set out along both of these lines. Make sure the grid is measured in the horizontal plane and grid points and diagonals are checked constantly throughout the excavation. Once the site grid is established, the marker pegs need to be labelled with their grid coordinates.

Usually a grid works — like on Ordnance Survey maps — on a system of easting measured from west to east, and northing measured from

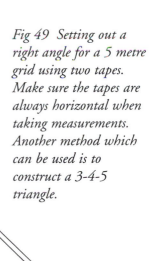

Tapes

7.07m

5.00m

7.07m

Baseline

5.00m

Fig 49 Setting out a right angle for a 5 metre grid using two tapes. Make sure the tapes are always horizontal when taking measurements. Another method which can be used is to construct a 3-4-5 triangle.

53533

south to north. Measurements start, again like Ordnance Survey maps, from the south-west corner of the site grid, which is called the point of origin.

In case you need in the future to extend the site grid to the west it is usual to start at the point of origin with 100E 300N (always label your easting from west to east). The next grid line intersection point to the east on a 5-metre grid will be 105E 300N, the next 110E 300N, the next 115E 300N etc. The grid points to the north of your point of origin will be 100E 305N, the next 100E 310N, the next 100E 315N the next 100E 320N etc. Sometimes sites are marked with an alpha-numeric system, A1, A2, A3 and B1, B2, B3; it really is a matter of choice and the level of precision needed.

If possible draw up a sketch plan clearly showing the site and its grid. Number the plan with the system of coordinates that you will be using. This will help archaeologists and students to become orientated to the site.

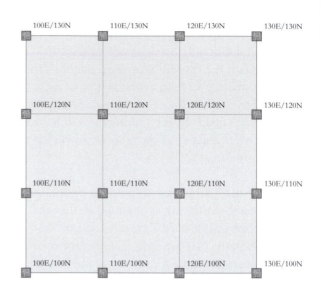

Fig 51 Mark your site grid with coordinates and make sure everybody has a copy. On some sites it is worthwhile to paint the top of the posts and write the coordinates on them.

Taking levels

A site grid exists in the horizontal plan only, and as the positions of contexts and plans must be recorded in three dimensions it is necessary to measure vertical heights or levels on site in relation to a known datum level. The known datum level has been established by the Ordnance Survey on the present sea level at Newlyn in Cornwall. The Ordnance Survey has established a nationwide grid of benchmarks that are marked with their heights on all large-scale maps

The machines for taking levels are called prismatic 'automatic' levels. Make sure it is sited at a spot from which the temporary benchmark (TBM) and the area to be surveyed can be seen.

Extend the tripod legs, spread the legs wide and ensure the tripod plate is almost on a level with your eye. Press the legs into the ground and make sure the tripod is firmly fixed and stable. Look and see if the tripod plate is horizontal; it is possible to check this with your line level.

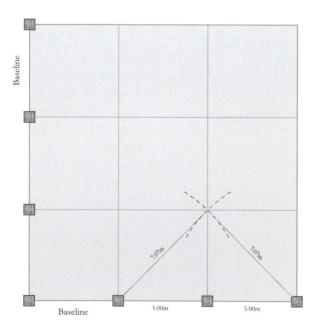

Fig 50 Extend the site grid from the baseline by tape, checking diagonals and ensuring the tapes are kept horizontal.

Raising or lowering the individual tripod legs will make changes to the level you are measuring.

Note also that with the use of GPS equipment there is no need for bench marks as the system will set its location from orbiting satellites. When the tripod is fixed firmly and stable, take the instrument out of its box and attach it to the top of the tripod.

The automatic level has a small circular bubble within a ring marked on glass. Ensure the bubble is within the inner circle by using the three large levelling screws at the base of the instrument to level it. Once it is level, turn the instrument through 90° and check the bubble is still within the inner circle. The site level or dumpy is now ready to use.

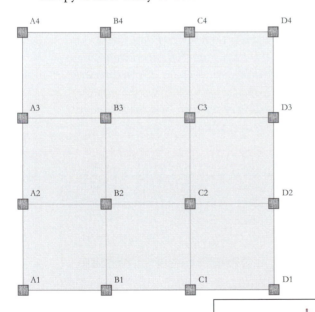

Fig 52 *Labelling your grid with an alpha-numeric system may be easier to use in teaching situations. It is also possible to lay out the site grid by using the degree bezel on the site level (right). To get a right-angle, turn the head 90 degrees.*

The survey staff

The survey staff is marked in paint with a large ruler divided into 1-centimetre squares; usually each alternate metre is coloured alternately in red or black. Extend the survey staff, ensuring the button on the back of it clicks firmly into position.

Ask an assistant to hold the staff vertically with its heel or base on the benchmark or TBM. Looking through the telescope, and noting the staff measurement against the horizontal cross-wire in the telescope, read the staff. Some site levels may have stadia lines in addition to the main cross wires running horizontally and vertically across the field of view. These stadia lines, usually two short horizontal lines equally spaced above and below the main horizontal lines, are used to measure distance but can lead to a mis-reading when you are levelling.

Ensure the staff is vertical by seeing that the vertical cross-wire in the telescope lines up with the vertical lines on the staff.

It will be necessary to arrange a simple code of signals with your assistant so that he or she can extend the staff if needed and keep it vertical. If the cross-wires are not clear, it is possible to alter the focus by rotating the eye piece. However for focusing on the staff, use the main focusing knob, which is usually located on the side of the instrument.

Once you have taken your reading against the horizontal cross-wire of the telescope, add this value to the level of the benchmark and you have the level of the cross-wire in the telescope. Now place the heel of the staff on the point whose level is required and take a new reading on the staff. Subtract this value from the level of the cross-wire and this figure will give the level of the new point. The addition and subtraction of staff

Ordnance Survey datum levels.
The benchmarks are usually cut into stone on permanent structures like churches, bridges and public buildings. These are an inverted 'V', like an arrow, with an incised line on top. The actual benchmark level is the horizontal incised line. All levels on site must be measured in relation to a fixed datum level of either a benchmark or more usually a TBM (temporary or transferred benchmark). To find out the height of a TBM it will be necessary to take a chain of levels from an Ordnance Survey benchmark

to the TBM and return to the OS benchmark in a closed traverse. The value at the end of the traverse should be the same as at the beginning, which will make the exercise self checking.

However, there is almost always a small discrepancy in heights that is usually acceptable. To minimise errors it is worthwhile to measure the half divisions on the survey staff, i.e. 5mm rather than 1cm (10mm), and to take readings to three decimal places of a metre.

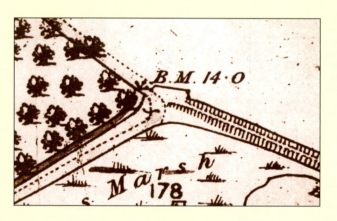

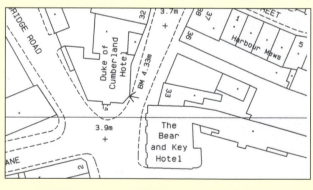

Fig 53 Ordnance Survey benchmarks appear on all OS maps of the appropriate scale. Modern maps are marked in a metric scale, (below left, at 4.33m) but the scale on earlier maps is imperial feet and inches. On this early map (left) of Milton near Sittingbourne, Kent, the benchmark is shown where it is incised into the fabric of the wall and the Ordnance Datum as shown is 14.0 feet.

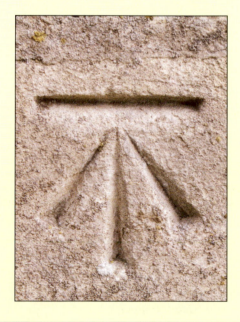

Fig 54 Photograph of an Ordnance Survey benchmark incised on to a church building at Teynham in Kent. The OD height can be found on large-scale OS maps or can be bought from Ordnance Survey. The datum point is taken from the centre of the top horizontal incised bar. Although marked on maps, it is sometimes difficult to find benchmarks on sites.

readings taken on known and unknown points is the essence of taking levels on archaeological sites. The first reading to the TBM is called a 'back sight'.

Additional readings on other points are called 'foresights'. Work out the height of your TBM above the Ordnance Survey known datum level, add the back sight figure to this and this will give the 'Instrument Height' (IH), which is the height of the horizontal cross-wires on your dumpy above the OS datum. Take the foresight readings and subtract each in turn from the instrument height. The results are the 'reduced levels', which give the height of each point above OS Chart datum. Write down the results on the site plan in this manner: 18.03m OD (Ordnance Datum).

Automatic optical levels are widely used for precise levelling in most areas of archaeological survey and are designed to fulfil the need of archaeologists who require a level that is very accurate, yet quick and simple to use. An automatic optical level consists of a high-quality telescope mounted on a precisely machined rotary base. A very stable, self-levelling compensator mechanism within the telescope provides an accurately levelled line of sight. Levels are determined and set out on site by measuring the height differences between any number of survey points.

A graduated rule or survey staff is positioned at the selected points, and the optical level is used to measure the relative height of each point. Set up the optical level on a tripod using the circular bubble on it to set the instrument approximately level. The internal levelling mechanism will now provide an accurate and automatically self-levelled line of optical sight.

Fig 55 The surveyor's assistant will need to hold the staff vertically whilst readings are taken. To read the scale it is best to remember that each thick coloured line (black or red) and white intervening space is a centimetre, and each 'E' shape is the equivalent of five centimetres in height.
Remember the centimetre 'cube' is your measurement, not the lines.
The level (right) shown is 0.61m.

Fig 56 Set up the tripod by spreading and pushing the legs into the ground. Extend the legs of the tripod until the base plate is roughly horizontal and at eye level. Screw on the instrument and centre the circular spirit level bubble by turning the levelling screws. Look along the instrument and locate the staff with the coarse sight located on top of the telescope. Look through the telescope and turn the coarse or fine focus wheel until the staff is clear and sharp. Turn the horizontal drive wheel to set the staff at the centre of your vision. You can now read the vertical measurement off the staff.

Angle measurement

Most automatic optical levels incorporate a scale in degrees on the rotating base that can be used to set out the 90° corners on the site grid. To set out an angle, the instrument is placed exactly above the proposed corner of the baseline using a plumb bob, and the telescope is aimed down the baseline. The degrees scale is then set to zero. The telescope can now be swept round to the required angle, which is read directly from off the graduated scale in 1° units.

Rotating laser levels

One of the main advantages of using a rotating laser level, when compared with an optical level, is that laser levelling is a one-person operation. The laser level is set up and the archaeologist can move around the site setting up levels single handedly, whereas with an optical level two people are required, one to hold the measuring staff and the other to take the readings.

Laser levels are also very simple to use and archaeologists need only a few minutes' instruction.

Using a rotating laser level

The rotating laser sweeps a level laser beam across the site and all measurements are related to the height of the beam. In subdued lighting conditions the moving spot of the laser beam will produce a level red line, but in bright sunlight it can be difficult to see the laser beam, so a detector unit or receiver is used to locate the

Fig 57 A student survey team at work in the field. For landscape survey or contour profiling it is necessary to set up a series of control points from which a set of triangulated horizontal measurements can be plotted in.

beam. The receiver consists of a laser sensor that detects the rotating laser beam, with an LCD display and bleeper that indicate the position of the laser beam as it moves.

The display has 'high' 'on target' and 'low' indicators. The bleeper also has different tones to indicate the laser position, which is very useful when working down in trenches, where the receiver up on a staff would be too high to read visually.

Laser levels that emit two laser beams, one at 90° to the other, can be used to set out the right angles needed on a site grid. Rotating laser levels can be set level either manually or are automatically self-levelling. The range of a laser level is dependent on the speed of beam rotation, the power of the laser and the sensitivity of the detector unit. However, some models have a range up to 800 metres.

EDM and total stations

The use of electronic equipment on

Fig 58 A typical automatic total station set up on its tripod. The circular bubble on the level is used to set the instrument approximately level. The internal levelling mechanism will now provide an accurate and automatically self-levelling line of sight.

Stadia lines

Most tacheometry automatic optical levels are provided with stadia lines, two short horizontal lines equally spaced above and below the main horizontal in the eyepiece. These stadia lines can be used to compute distance in a method of surveying which is called tacheometry. The process is simple. Look through the telescope and sight on the staff. Read the staff reading on the top stadia line, and read the staff reading on the bottom stadia line. Subtract the low reading from the high and multiply by one hundred:

Distance = (2·50m - 2.00m)= 0.50m x 100 =50m

Alternatively, if the mathematics proves to be a little difficult, count the number of centimetres from the lower reading to the top reading on the staff. In this case it would be 50cm = 50 metres, i.e. every one centimetre on the staff would equal one metre in distance.

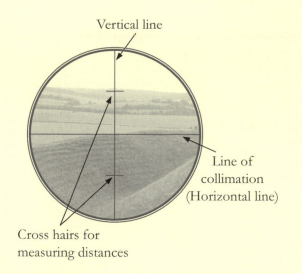

Vertical line

Line of collimation (Horizontal line)

Cross hairs for measuring distances

Fig 59 Typical cross hairs (stadia lines) seen through the eyepiece of the site level telescope showing above and below the main vertical/horizontal cross-wires.

archaeological sites is increasing rapidly. EDM and Total Station equipment is now so easy to use that any archaeologist with a few hours' training will be able to carry out all of the surveying operations described in this book. The only drawback is the cost of the equipment, although for large projects it may be worthwhile hiring it for the duration of the job.EDM (Electronic Distance Measurement) was first developed to enhance the capabilities of a theodolite, and known as a Total Station, the EDM records all the survey data digitally. Then the EDM can, through the appropriate software and if sufficient points have been being taken, print a plan of the site with contour profiling. The EDM is set up on a tripod and when switched on the built-in transmitter sends out a

beam, usually infra-red, which is returned by the reflector held at the point needed for survey.

The beam is in a wave form and when it arrives back at the transmitter a comparison is made between the times of waves going out and the waves coming back. From this data the speed and time of travel is found and the distance computed.

The data can be affected by variations in atmospheric temperature and pressure and correction has to be applied using reliable values for temperature and pressure.

The EDM can be used for setting out site grids but area surveys are its forte. The relationship between heights and distances and the location of the EDM are recorded and a large area can be surveyed in this way, certainly up to three kilometres depending on conditions.

To undertake a survey, set up the EDM on a spot where most, if not all, of the area to be surveyed can be seen. All the points to be surveyed are located and numbered using the codes specified by the software. The software programme should be suitable for drawing various types of features — earthworks, buildings, roads and trees.

The Total Station has the capacity to record a large number of three dimensional coordinates that can be used to construct landscape models in two or three dimensions.

Surveying with GPS
The Global Positioning System is such a flexible technique that it can be applied to most traditional surveying tasks. GPS is now the principal technique used by surveyors, map makers and organisations such as English Heritage to position features accurately on a map or plan.

The majority of archaeological surveyors have up to now been using surveying techniques based on the theodolite, EDM, plane-tables, tapes and

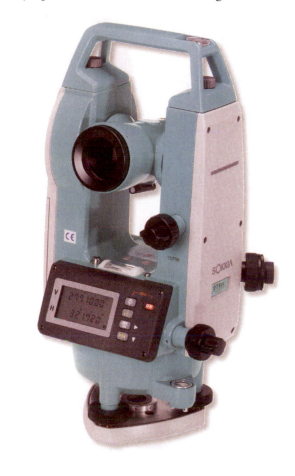

Fig 60 The digital electronic theodolite is used to measure horizontal and vertical angles with ease. All measurements are shown on the electronic display panel and can be saved and downloaded into an appropriate software programme.

offset, grids and other equipment. GPS is one of the latest surveying techniques with its own advantages and disadvantages. As a means of providing a fast and accurate location of points on the earth's surface it has no rival when used correctly and subject to the right conditions.

However, it is best to recognise that GPS is only one of many survey tools available and on some sites other methods of survey may be quicker and more efficient. The site topography will need to be assessed to see if there are any constraints on using GPS.

The most obvious is that it is difficult to operate GPS in heavily wooded areas. Locating the position of an archaeological feature on an Ordnance Survey map has always been one of the most fundamental requirements of the archaeological record and GPS is one of the best methods of achieving this. Positioning is instant, simple and reliable, and no other surveying method can achieve the same speed, reliability, accuracy or cost efficiency. Whereas previously, surveying was governed by line of sight along the ground, GPS has removed that constraint and all that is necessary is to be able to 'see' the sky and most GPS units will tell the operator if a 'fix' has been established with sufficient

Fig 61 A survey-grade GPS machine being used by Stewart Ainsworth of English Heritage.

height information.

Mapping-grade GPS:
Map accuracy and absolute accuracy down to 1m can be achieved, in real-time or if post-processed. Suitable for mapping up to 1:25,000 scale but not suitable for site survey.

Survey-grade GPS:
Centimetre relative accuracy. Map accuracy and absolute accuracy to the nearest centimetre can be achieved in real time or by post-processing.

However, a poor survey cannot be made more accurate by using a good map base, although a good survey on a poor map base is potentially more useful. At each stage an assessment of the factors affecting accuracy should be made and noted. Further details on the array of services and information on how to carry out surveying with GPS in Britain can be obtained through www.gps.gov.uk

satellites orbiting the earth to obtain the correct position and height. GPS equipment can be grouped under three types of equipment:

Navigation-grade GPS:
Map accuracy and absolute accuracy approximately c.10m. Good for finding location in relation to maps and relocating sites, but not suitable for site survey, also notoriously bad for

Scale change
Occasionally it is necessary to change the scale of maps and drawings. It may be necessary to photocopy at least twice to obtain the new scale. However do not forget the finished photocopy will only be an approximate of the scale required and is not to be used for survey work.

It is advisable to draw a scale bar on the original drawing so that the reduction or enlargement can be checked for accuracy.

English Heritage technical papers.

There are a number of publications that English Heritage provide free of charge on aspects of archaeology. The most important are: *With Alidade and Tape: Graphical and plane table survey of archaeological earthworks,* written by Mark Bowden, one of the most experienced practioners in his field; and *Where on Earth are We? The Global Positioning System (GPS) in archaeological field survey,* written by Stewart Ainsworth and Benard Thomason.

Stewart Ainsworth is better known for his work with Time-Team. Other papers from English Heritage include *Environmental Archaeology: A guide to the theory and practice of methods, from sampling and recovery to post-excavation*; and *Human Bones from Archaeological Sites.*

Both are produced by the Centre of Archaeology and available free of charge from English Heritage, 37 Tanner Row, York YO1 6WP e-mail: rachel.ashcroft@english-heritage.org.uk. Thanks is given to English Heritage for the use of photographs, written information and survey data.

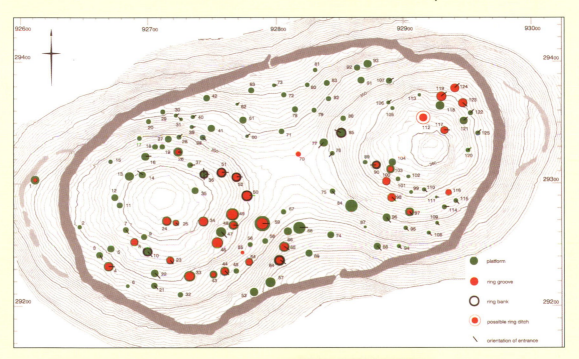

platform
ring groove
ring bank
possible ring ditch
orientation of entrance

A typical real-time, survey-grade GPS equipment in use at Norham Castle, Northumberland, by English Heritage. You will find on a development site that whilst archaeologists talk in centimetres no other surveyor will. All measurements are in millimetres, indeed it is recognised that centimetres are not a recognised measure — but try telling that to an archaeologist!

Contour model by English Heritage of the topography of Yeavering Bell, Northumberland, derived from survey-grade GPS. (English Heritage).

CHAPTER SIX: THE DRAWN RECORD

'The recording of archaeological sites discovered in the field essentially has three elements: a written description of the site, a survey including plans and elevations and a photographic record'
(Field Archaeology: An Introduction, P. Drewett, 1999).

Survey can be divided into two areas of archaeological activity: first, the recording of large sites and landscapes (Chapter Three), and secondly, as shown in this chapter, the laying out of grids and trenches to serve as a framework within which features and contexts can be located, excavated and recorded.
It is essential to use the correct scale appropriate to the job in hand; it is pointless recording any structure to 1 millimetre, as it is impossible to record such small measurements on a drawing.

All drawings should be measured in the field to the appropriate scale and recorded on plastic film. Tracing paper, despite its lower cost, is not stable enough to use. Most recording on plastic film is done with a 4H to 7H pencil with a preference for 6H, which will need to be constantly sharpened. It may be appropriate to use coloured pencils to differentiate different materials, but it is unlikely that coloured drawings will make it to publication in Britain, although European archaeologists record and publish extensively in colour. Plastic film comes in a variety of thicknesses and finishes. The most useful for archaeological drawing is the translucent drawing film called Permatrace in 150 micron or 0.0005-inch thickness. It is worth remembering that survey or 'data capture systems' are changing rapidly and many archaeological organisations are switching to use

electronic pen maps which can electronically store the information digitally.

A planning board is necessary; the best are made of white plastic laminate and can be mounted on to a tripod. For excavation planning it is

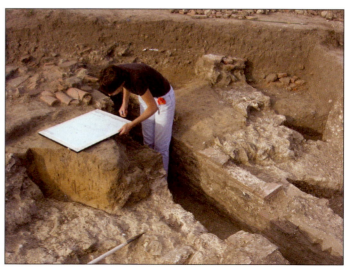

Fig 62 The keeping of the Site Archive is of paramount importance. Here detailed 1:20 plans are being drawn of a Roman octagonal bath-house excavated by the KAFS.

essential to have a laminated sheet of metric graph paper fixed to the planning board. The plastic film is attached over this, and your scale drawing can utilise the metric graph.

The aim of all surveys is to make a scale plan on film of what needs to be recorded on site. A excavation site plan is normally plotted at a scale of 1:100; 1 metre on the ground is equivalent to 1 centimetre (10mm) on the scaled plan. It is expected that any object over 10 centimetres (100mm) in size be recorded.

A site plan is necessary on every site where contexts are recorded. It has two purposes; one, to locate the archaeological information, such as the site grid and the location of section and elevation drawings, and secondly the location of the site externally in relation to the OS. A lot of archaeological detail is lost on such a small scale, and for more complex sites a scale of 1:50 is sometimes used. At 1:50, 50 centimetres

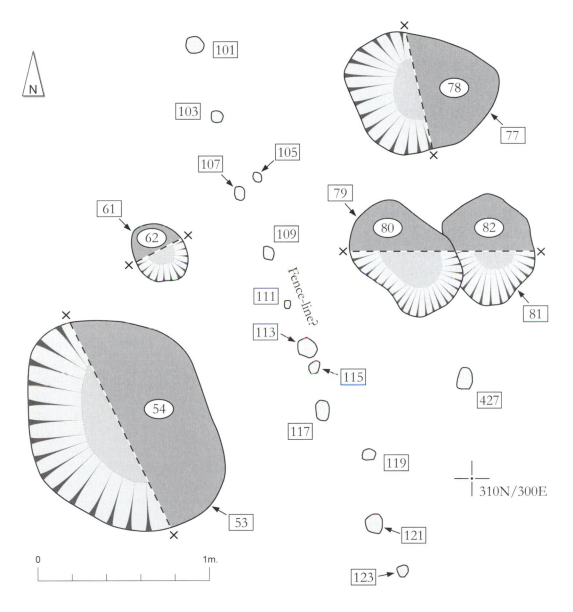

Fig 63 The multi-context plan has more than one context recorded. Section drawings are recorded by x-x. Drawn in is the site grid here showing coordinates 310N/300E, the metric scale and north. The large pit 53 is shown sectioned and hachures indicate the shape.
Make sure you take trianglulated measurements from at least three grid pegs.

(500mm) on the ground equals 1 centimetre (10mm) on the scale plan. It would be expected that any object over 5 centimetres (50mm) in size would be recorded. A scale of 1:50 can also be used to record large sections.

The scale of 1:20 is the standard scale for recording contexts, and it is possible to plot on to an A3 plastic film sheet an area of 5 x 5 metres that will represent the 5-metre site survey grid used on most archaeological sites. It would be expected that any object over 2 centimetres (20mm) in size would be drawn.

For drawing sections, elevations, cremations and any small deposits, the scale of 1:10 is used. Ten centimetres on the ground is equivalent to 1 centimetre on the scale plan. At this scale every object over 1 centimetre in size can be drawn, although it is often a waste of time and unnecessary. 1:1 or same size is only used for the recording of decoration, inscriptions or mosaics and is seldom used on site.

Planning

At every stage of an archaeological excavation a plan is made to show the location of features and contexts or layers. These plans provide a permanent record of the archaeology that is being removed by excavation. It is essential that people starting in archaeology acquire the skills necessary to fulfil this obligation. The plan needs to be surveyed into its surrounding site grid to locate it horizontally. Levels need to be taken to locate the plan vertically. The levels should be written on to the plan, and the plan

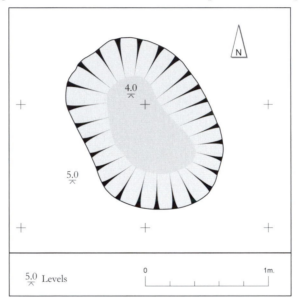

Fig 64 Single-context plan showing spot-heights on a datum symbol, hachures and metric scale.

must also be indexed into the site archive. There are two different drawing systems in use on archaeological sites: multi-context planning (Fig 63) and single-context planning (Fig 64). Multi-context planning has more than one context drawn on one plan. Usually the entire site is drawn as a series of area plans based on the site grid of 5- or 10-metre squares.

It may be worthwhile to draw the site at 1:20 scale as a pre-excavation plan and then a post-excavation plan with appropriate sections. For complex sites it will be necessary to use the method of planning developed by the Museum of London Archaeological Services (MoLAS) and called Single-Context Planning. On a single-context plan and excavation every single context has its own plan (Fig 64). Other features, such as cut ditches and large post-holes, may occasionally include a section drawing. The single-context planning system is ideal for recording the stratigraphic sequence of a complex urban site that has been formed by stratified deposition and has areas of subsequent truncation.

Contexts

Up to the 1970s the Wheeler/Kenyon system of archaeological recording was prevalent, with trenches being given Roman numerals and layers of deposition an Arabic number — e.g. Trench VI, layer 6. Ed Harris, working at the Lower Brook Street site in Winchester, had the unenviable task of trying to correlate the stratigraphical data of a complex urban site recorded in site notebooks to the method used by Wheeler and Kenyon. Harris quickly discovered that the traditional method of recording was inadequate and suggested a pro-forma, the so-called Context Sheet, where each deposit or cut or structure was numbered with its own unique number.

Stratification

Stratification is the superimposition of layers of

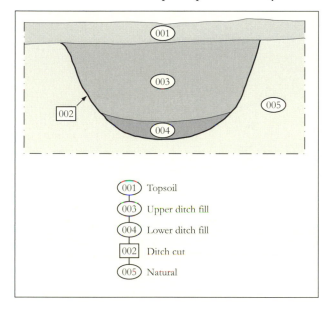

Fig 65 *From the section drawing it is possible to see that just below the topsoil a ditch was cut (002) into the natural soil (005) and open long enough to be silted (004). The ditch was then filled up (003) and a deposit of topsoil formed over the top of the ditch (001).*

deposits one on top of each other through time. To understand and record a site, archaeologists will strip off the layers (contexts) starting from the surface, which is, of course, the latest layer. Artefacts found in each of these contexts will date that context. Coins will relatively date the pottery, which in turn can relatively date animal bones, walls, floors etc.

On earlier prehistoric sites absolute dating can

be obtained by a variety of scientific procedures including Radio-carbon or C14 dating, whilst on Roman, medieval and other sites surviving timber can be absolutely dated by dendrochronology. Each context is issued with its own unique number. This number will also identify any artefact or indeed ecofact removed from that context. In addition, cuts for rubbish pits or building foundations are also given a unique number.

The Harris matrix

In recording the stratification of a site by using the single-context recording system a large number of separate pro-formas and plans are produced. To make sense of this mass of data, Ed Harris devised the Harris Matrix, which provides a simple method of relating one context to another according to the relative stratigraphy and sequence of deposition or removal of each. Every deposit and cut is given its own

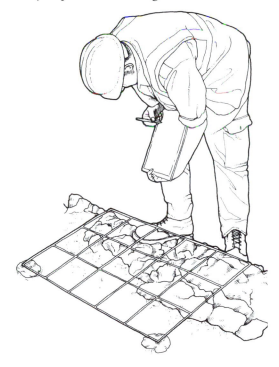

Fig 66 *Illustration showing the use of a planning frame. Make sure the frame is horizontal and if necessary prop up the corners before drawing the feature to be recorded.*

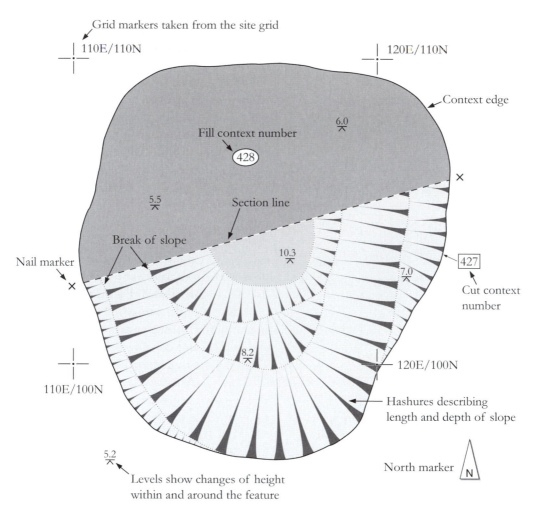

Grid markers taken from the site grid

110E/110N

120E/110N

Context edge

Fill context number

428

6.0

5.5

Section line

Break of slope

10.3

Nail marker

7.0

427

Cut context number

120E/100N

8.2

110E/100N

Hashures describing length and depth of slope

5.2

North marker

Levels show changes of height within and around the feature

Fig 67 Plan of a large pit, a single feature showing levels, hachures, section drawing line (x-x), site grid, and context numbers.

unique number. On the pro-forma single-context recording sheet for a cut all the numbered layers of stratification contained within that cut may be listed. This will give invaluable information to specialists about the contexts of finds and will show which finds can be grouped together. A site matrix can be constructed showing the logical relationships between deposits, and these relationships can be built up into an overall site sequence. One of the easiest ways to construct a Harris Matrix is to treat each context number as an historical event. These events interact to form the Matrix, the site's time-line.

Drawing the plan

Each plan must have a site code, a context number if a single context, the north sign, the scale used, and the date of the drawing and the name of the planner. Detailed areas of fallen masonry, buried pits and skeletons are drawn by laying a planning frame over the feature and drawing it a square at a time.

The easiest way to acquire a good planning frame is to purchase a 1-metre square piece of reinforcing steel mesh from a builders' merchants. The mesh is divided into a 20-centimetre grid. At 1:20 scale each 1-centimetre square on the graph paper equals one 20-centimetre square of the planning frame. Mark the 5-metre square site grid and its

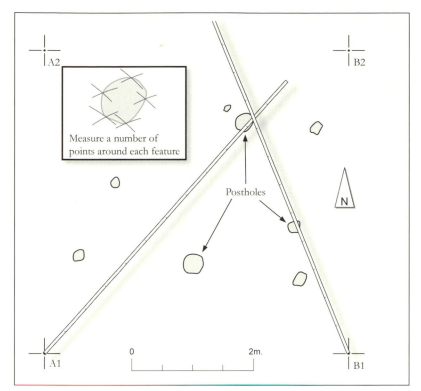

Fig 68 *The location of features within the site grid can be plotted by attaching two tapes to two separate grid points and crossing over the tapes on the point of the feature to be recorded.*
An additional check can be done with a third tape.
Make sure tapes are kept horizontal.

attached to the nail and lay it across the tape stretched between the two grid points.

Swing the tape slowly in an arc and when you have the smallest measurement on the swung tape you will have found the right angle and correct distance between the tape stretched between the two grid points and the tape attached to the nail.

Triangulation

Triangulation is one of the better methods used to record the exact location of features within the area of the site grid. Attach a tape measure to two of the grid points and cross over the tapes on the feature to be recorded. It is essential to keep the tapes taut and horizontal. If necessary use a plumb bob to mark the point to be measured. Read the length on both tapes.

Meanwhile the second person, who is drawing, should position the point of his compass at the spot on the plastic film corresponding (in scale) to the exact position of one of the grid points. Next, set the compass at the scale measure equal to the length of the tape and draw an arc.

Repeat the procedure for the second grid point. Where the two arcs intersect is the location of the point to be plotted. Follow the same procedure for plotting all the points needed round the feature and join up the dots by freehand drawing, if necessary by using a planning frame, but certainly by looking closely at the feature whilst drawing it.

Before the feature is removed by archaeologists, it will be necessary to ascertain its height, using the site level. Once the vertical position and height are known they should be marked down on your plan.

co-ordinates on to the plastic film and lightly mark the interior of the square at 5-centimetre intervals.

These points are where the 1-metre planning frame should be positioned; if it is felt unnecessary to draw with the planning frame it will be necessary to measure the features using measuring tapes.

There are a number of methods — offsetting is often used — but for ease of working triangulation is the preferred method. If offsetting with tapes, a tape is stretched between two grid points along the grid line. Place a nail, with a tape attached, at the point on the feature you wish to record. To offset, take the tape

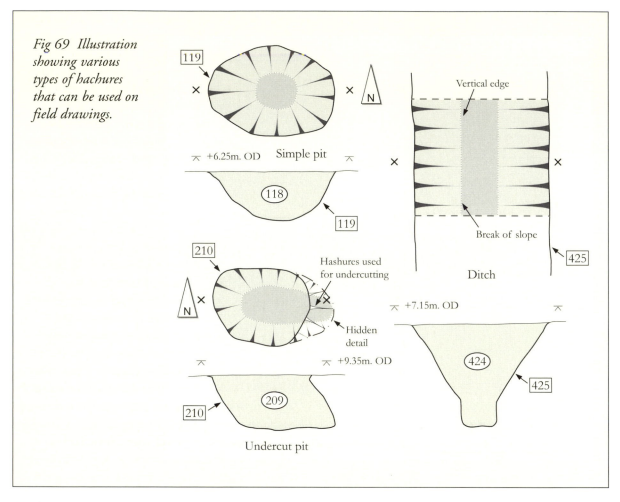

Fig 69 Illustration showing various types of hachures that can be used on field drawings.

Hachures

The conventions of hachures are used on drawings to show the surface undulation of an archaeological site (see Fig 72). Banks and ditches can be highlighted by hachures to emphasise the slight variations of a slope; the closer the hachure, the steeper the slope. The length of the hachure will show the length of the slope. Each hachure has a triangular top that is always drawn in at the top of the slope, and at the break in angle at the bottom of the slope is shown as a dotted line.

Excavation edges, sections and baulks are not illustrated by hachures. If the edge is vertical, tail-less hachures are shown and, if it is undercutting the break of a slope, it is indicated with a dot-line-dot.

Section drawing

A section drawing records the vertical stratification of a site, whilst a profile drawing records a deposit that cannot be sectioned. Elevation drawings record standing walls or buildings found on site. A running section placed across the site records vertically deposits as they are removed, and it will need to be continuously updated. The scale of section drawings is usually 1:10, 10 centimetres on the ground equals 1 centimetre on the scale plan. It is essential that a large enough board and sheet of plastic film be used. If the section is too big for one sheet of film, split the section equally between two drawings and make sure they match. Conversely if the section is small it may be appropriate to bundle all the sections on one sheet of film.

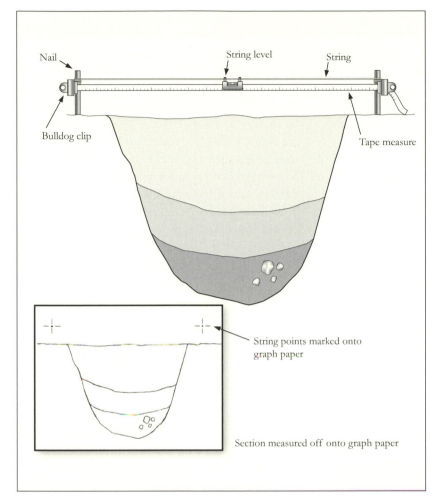

Fig 70 *How to set up a section drawing. Make sure the vertical measurements are taken from the stretched horizontal string and not the tape measure.*

Setting up a section

It is usual to set a nail on one side of the section and to stretch a piece of string tightly along the section making sure the string is level by either checking with the site dumpy or by using a line level. This is a small spirit level with two hooks that allow it to be suspended from a horizontal piece of string to ensure the string is absolutely horizontal.

It is essential that the line level be hung at one end of the string; if hung in the centre it may cause the string to sag. When the string is level,

the second nail can be placed in position and a tape is attached to the nails with bulldog clips or clothes pegs. This will provide the horizontal scale. Vertical readings are taken with a second tape at appropriate points of the section. Once drawn to scale they will provide dots on the drawing that then can be joined up whilst looking at the section.

An easier way to set up is to use a plastic builders' level in the appropriate size; they are made in 1-, 2-, 3- and 4-metre lengths. Tap in one 6-inch nail and place the builders' level on top. The instrument's bubble will tell you when it is level, then tap in the second nail. Secure the level with elastic bands if windy. On top of the level is printed a metric measure, and because the level is rigid, a 3-metre or 5-metre tape will hook on top. The plastic or metal case of the tape measure will act as a plumb bob, and it is an easy task to read off both the horizontal and vertical measurements from both sets of tapes. The height or depth of the string or builders' level needs to be recorded using the site level, and the location of the section needs to be drawn on the site plan by using either the offset or triangulation method. If the section is wide and the string long it may be necessary to set up a horizontal line of nails using either the site level or one of the new generations of laser levels.

In open area excavations, where layers are completely removed one at a time, it may be necessary to plot the thickness of the layers and their relationship to each other by drawing the height of each new deposit as it is exposed.

It is essential that two sturdy posts are set up at the beginning of the excavation that will last throughout the duration of the excavation. Remove the string and tape after each measuring session, as they will impede access across the site.

It is worthwhile remembering that the position of the section must always be accurately plotted on to the site plan or the relevant context plan. Also keep in mind the following for all survey work:

1. Numbering: Section and elevation drawings should have their own numbering system.

2. Scale: Always write down the scale used.
3. Compass bearings: At either end of the section drawing the cardinal points should be written down. This is a safer method of recording than writing 'south facing section'.
4. Contexts: The limits of the contexts need to be clearly drawn with the appropriate line convention, and the context number marked on the context area and enclosed in a rectangular box for cuts and circular or oval for fills. Always draw in cuts using a solid line.
5. Datum points: Mark the levels on your drawing in relation to drawn points. The positions of the surveyed levels should be marked with the datum point symbol (Fig. 64).

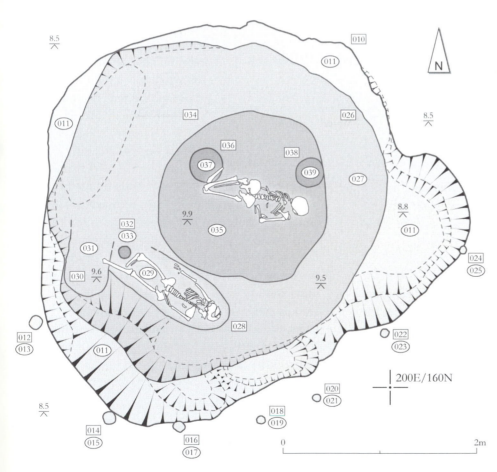

Fig 71 A typical plan drawing of an Iron Age hut excavated at Trinity Square, Margate, Kent, and recorded by the KAFS. Archaeological photographs were taken at every stage, but it is clear that a drawing can add a tremendous amount of detail which may not be obvious in the photographic record. The sunken hut, unusual in Iron Age Britain, held the remains of two individuals. One, a young man, had his head replaced at the time of burial by that of a much older man.

Fig 72 Hachures.
The concept of hachures is well understood by most archaeologists. It is a convention of many years' standing to illustrate the three dimensions on a two-dimensional drawing.
The triangular end of the hachure lies at the top of the slope whilst the length of the hachure shows the length of the slope. The closer the hachures, the steeper the slope. The other symbols are all used by archaeologists on site drawings.

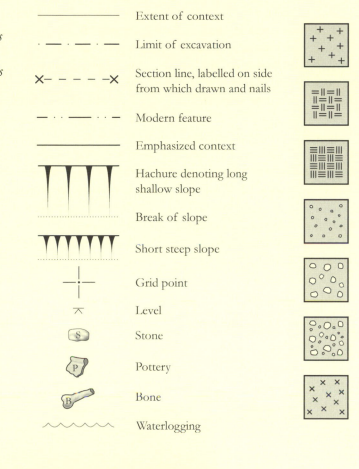

Extent of context

Limit of excavation

Section line, labelled on side from which drawn and nails

Modern feature

Emphasized context

Hachure denoting long shallow slope

Break of slope

Short steep slope

Grid point

Level

Stone

Pottery

Bone

Waterlogging

Charcoal

Clay 1

Clay 2

Sand

Gravel

Sand & Gravel

Mortar

Fig 73 The Time Team survey team in action.
From left to right, Stewart Ainsworth, Tony Wilmott (English Heritage), Neil Holbrook, Paul Wilkinson, Guy de la Bedoyere, Phil Harding, Malcolm Lyne, Carenza Lewis look at the landscape survey of Syndale, the site of the Roman town of Durolevum, for the TV programme on the possible early Roman fort which may be or may be not there.

CHAPTER SEVEN: THE WRITTEN RECORD

'The Site Recording Sheet is of paramount importance to the site records because it is the primary means of cross-referencing all the relevant information' *(Archaeological Site Manual, Museum of London, 1994).*

The Site Recording Sheet or Context Sheet is essential to the written archaeological record. Each distinct part of an archaeological feature — the cut of a ditch or the separate fills — will receive a unique context number. Each and every context number will generate a Context Sheet on which is described not only the physical feature but also its interpretation by the excavator.

Once the context is removed by excavation the Context Sheet is the primary surviving source of information on that destroyed archaeology. It is essential both to the person who is writing up the site and also to future archaeologists who may be able to re-interpret the function of the site using techniques as yet unknown.

Although there will be a wide variety of contexts found on an archaeological site the majority will be either cuts or deposits. Cuts will include pits, ditches, graves and foundation trenches for buildings. Deposits will include road and floor surfaces, pit, ditch, and grave fills as well as more complex features such as hearths, stone and timber buildings.

How to complete a Context Sheet

Every archaeological unit has its own Context Sheet but the information needed is usually the same. It consists of:

Site code: This will usually comprise a three-letter code and two numbers denoting the year of the excavation. For instance the excavation of the Roman town of Durolevum at Syndale would be SYN 07 whilst the excavation of the Roman Villa at Deerton Street would be DST 07.

Grid square(s): The site grid is established with the point of origin outside and to the south-west of all the areas of archaeological activity. The grid is usually laid out in 5- or 10-metre squares identified by the co-ordinates of their south-west corners.

Context number: A context number is allocated to each and every separate component of an archaeological feature. For instance, a posthole

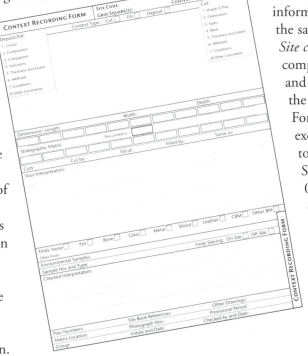

Fig 74 An example of a Context Recording Sheet.

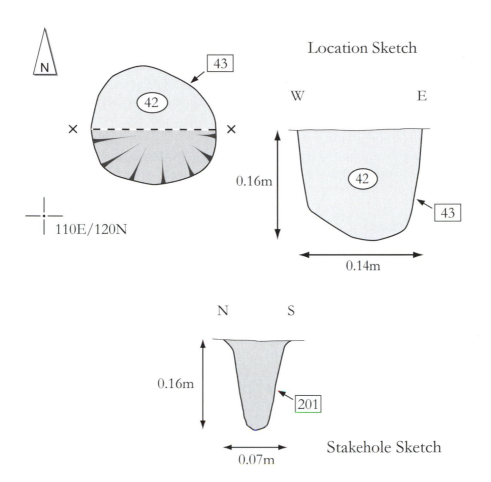

Location Sketch

N

42

43

× ×

110E/120N

W   E

0.16m

42

43

0.14m

N   S

0.16m

201

0.07m

Stakehole Sketch

Fig 75 If you are recording a posthole, or indeed any feature on the Context Recording Sheet, make sure a location sketch (left) and section (right) are added to the back of the Context Sheet.

may have up to five numbers — a cut number for the posthole, post packing, post pipe, post pipe cut, and possibly the backfill. These unique numbers record the events in the history of that posthole.

The sequence of numbers for each site normally start at 001 and the numbering is usually continuous. Context numbers are issued from a Context Register and should be obtained at the time of taking the Context Sheet.

Occasionally there can be confusion over the issuing of numbers, for instance in multiple ditch sections. It is valuable to remember that any newly excavated area must have its unique

set of numbers, if only to identify the finds found in context. Likewise some archaeologists prefer not to number modern features, but these are as likely as not to have impacted on the archaeology, and it is essential that they do have their context numbers — if in doubt number!

Context type

There are three main types of context numbers, all of which are enclosed in a unique frame on all drawings; these are deposits, cuts and structures. Deposits of soil are shown with an oval frame drawn around the context number but on the Context Sheet are annotated as 'deposit'. It is important to describe all contexts in the order of the prompts printed on the

Context Sheet. Following the order is necessary so that contexts can be compared with each other; it is also important that the information can be entered into a computer programme during post-excavation work.

Number each part of the deposit description to avoid confusion. The description of the soil will need to record its colour, any inclusions and its texture and composition.

Most pre-printed Context Sheets use a standardised vocabulary that will limit the options. Cuts are shown on all drawings by a rectangular frame drawn round the context number. It will be necessary once the description of a cut is completed to draw a measured profile

of the cut on the reverse of the Context Sheet. Describe the shape of the cut, its dimensions and depth, how the top of the cut breaks into the sides, the angle of the sides and the break of slope at the base. How is the base cut? Is it truncated and how much of its original shape survives? List all deposit context numbers which fill the cut. Structures are labelled on all drawings as a square apexed bracket around the context number. These will include walls, hearths, kilns and occasionally roads. It is usual for masonry structures to be recorded on a Masonry Recording Sheet, which will be explained more fully in Chapter Eight.

Stratigraphic matrix

Write the context number in the central box on

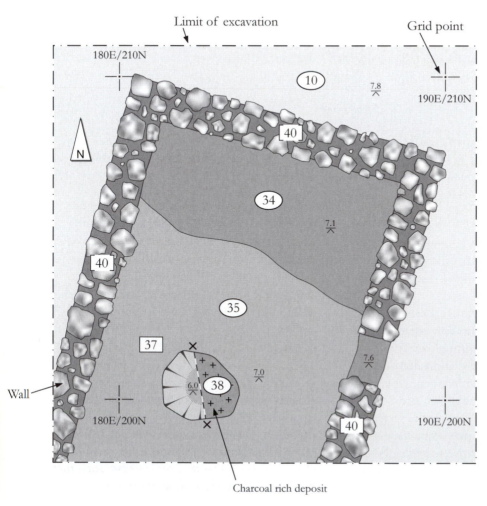

Fig 76 Part of a site plan showing the site grid and masonry foundations with other features drawn in. Levels are usually taken to two decimal places for accuracy and illustrate changes of height within and around the feature. Context numbers are circled by an oval for a fill, a rectangle for cuts and structures by square brackets.

the Context Sheet. Each context number needs to be treated as an historical event. These events shape the site matrix, which is the time-line of the site. Remember that the most recent event is at the top of the matrix and the earliest lies at the bottom.

Interpretation: It is only necessary to write an appropriate interpretation. Is it a pit, ditch, floor or midden?

Discussion: Start with a brief description of the context type: e.g. 'lower fill of ditch 98'. Add why you have come to this conclusion and describe the evidence, also cross-referencing the

Context Recording Sheet.

Photographs can provide slides for lectures and publication, and both colour slides and prints show some of the more complex features to be found on a site.

Digital still and video photography has added a new dimension to photographing archaeology, as many hundreds of images can be stored electronically and utilised for reports. Good publicity photographs are needed for the press and other media.

It is essential that major finds and discoveries are

Fig 77 Students of the KAFS excavating part of a timber Roman building alongside Watling Street in Kent.

context with the available information from the site: e.g. 'Ditch curves to the east and abuts the standing church building'. Write down the numbers of any section or elevation drawings that contain the context number.

Photographs: Taking photographs on site is usually looked upon as ancillary to the recording process and not an integral part of it. This is unfortunate as photographs can enhance the drawn record. It is necessary to record the film and frame numbers of the photograph on the

Fig 78 A photograph of a Roman fluted column built into the fabric of an Anglo-Saxon church at Newnham in Kent. The cm. scale ruler has been stuck to the wall with blu-tak.

Fig 79 A KAFS excavation at Star Hill, Bridge, in progress. Individual archaeologists are posing in excavated Anglo-Saxon graves to indicate how the graves had been cut into an earlier feature, a unique hexagonal ditch with a central, circular burial pit. All three graves contained seventh century burials, the grave goods included gold jewellery, glass cups, spears, silver coins, and daggers.

made known to the general public at the appropriate time, as public support for archaeology is important. General views of the site can be taken from a scaffolding tower, and for the best results the site must be kept tidy and 'photogenic' at all times. Colours can be enhanced on sections by spraying with water, the surrounding grass will need to be kept tidy and clipped. All photographs must include a scale in the form of either a ranging rod or a purpose-made photographic scale, unless they are to be used for publicity in which case a person should be included to give a scale. Digital video is now being used more frequently on site. The best use of it is as a video diary recording exciting discoveries and developments on a day-to-day basis.

Levels: On the back of the Context Sheet write the value of the temporary bench mark (TBM) and the back sight. Add the two values together to get the instrument height in metres above Ordnance Datum (OD). Enter the foresight values in the box provided, marked (FS), and subtract these from the instrument height.

Environmental samples: Make a note on the Context Sheet of any environmental samples taken and the number of boxes.

Finds: Tick the appropriate boxes of finds found within the context. It is worth remembering that if numerous finds are discovered, you should describe the number and type of each find in the basic context description. This will provide information during the post-excavation analysis of contexts with numerous finds to enable dating to be done.

Specific finds like coins should be entered on the line below (see also Chapter Eleven/Twelve).

Location drawing: On the back of the Context Sheet, sketch in the location of the context with at least three grid points and the measured distances (see Fig. 75). Make sure north is at the top of the drawing and the dimensions of the context are added. When recording a cut, draw a section and plan with measurements added. The Context Sheet should now be checked by the supervisor and signed and dated.

Flow diagram:

These stages must be completed when using the Context Recording System.

1. Clean area of context.
2. Identify the extent of context.
3. Ask if photographs are needed, and if so ensure the context is cleaned for photography
4. Find out the grid square co-ordinates for the feature.
5. Draw a plan of the context on plastic film at a scale of 1:20 or the appropriate scale.
6. Obtain a context number from the site context register and a Context Sheet.
7. Record the context number on the plans.
8. Ask for, or take, levels, mark the spot heights on the plan and write down the back sight and foresights on the back of the Context Sheet.
9. Ask for or reduce levels to OD and write on to the plan.
10. Write the description of the context on the Context Sheet.
11. Prepare a finds bag and label and mark on both the site code and context number.
12. Excavate the context.
13. Bag all finds and place in a secure place.
14. Overlay the plan with previous context plans to enable the stratigraphy to be understood.
15. Cross-reference the contexts on the Context Sheet and fill in the Matrix boxes.
16. Initial and date the plan and Context Sheet and pass on for checking by the Site Supervisor.

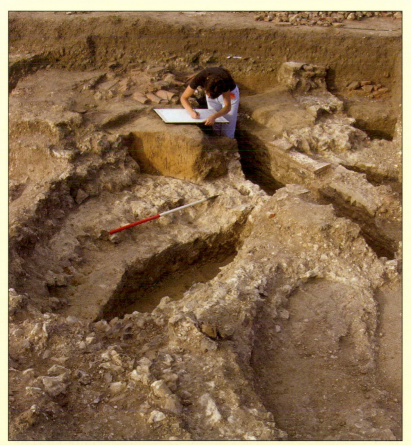

Fig 80 Recording in progress of an octagonal Roman bath house at Bax Farm in Kent. The structure has an outer wall, internal buttresses and a central octagonal plunge bath surrounded by a variety of other bathing facilities. The archaeologist from the KAFS is measuring the Roman brick hypocaust flue channel using a drawing frame and recording sections and plan on to a drawing board with a plastic film overlay. At the same time Context Sheets are filled in and digital and film photographs taken.

CHAPTER EIGHT: RECORDING STONE AND TIMBER

'The excavation and interpretation of stone buried walls and foundations appear at first sight to be easier than that of timber buildings.
If anything they are more difficult.'
(Techniques of Archaeological Excavation, Philip Barker, 1982).

According to Philip Barker the fundamental principles of all excavations should be to remove and record each layer or feature in the reverse order from that in which it was deposited, over as extensive an area as possible. He also notes that on occasions this ideal must be modified. One of these occasions is the presence of standing walls, which may complicate the recording and interpretation processes.

When the tops of walls are uncovered by excavation the layers of stratification are separated by the walls, and the site divides itself into smaller room-sized areas, which are usually dug separately. You should take out the construction trench layers (fills) then the wall. Any differences in types of masonry, stone, mortar and the construction details must be meticulously recorded and in the majority of cases a stone-by-stone drawing undertaken. MoLAS and other units have pioneered the recording of masonry structures and utilise a Masonry Recording Sheet. It is acknowledged that once walls are removed, the field record will become the primary source of information for the future study of that particular building.
The basic information that is needed from a

masonry structure includes its stratigraphic location and its form within the area of the excavation. From the data recorded it may be possible to draw an isometric projection of the structure and be able to date the various construction phases. To enable researchers to undertake these tasks it is necessary to record every element of the masonry structure on a Masonry Recording Sheet. The structure will have its own unique context numbers and general description written on a Context Recording Sheet (see Chapter Six). It will need to be drawn at 1:20 in plan and 1:10 in elevation and section and every worked stone recorded at 1:1. Samples of the mortar and any internal or external rendering will need to be taken plus samples of brick types and a sample of each different type of stone. Roofing tiles, bricks and floor tiles are usually called ceramic building materials, and will need to

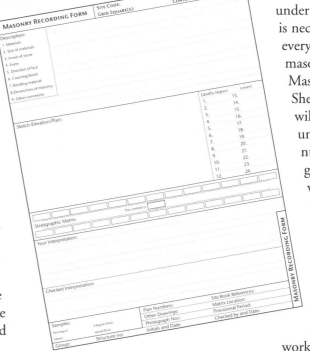

Fig 81 A Masonry Recording Sheet.

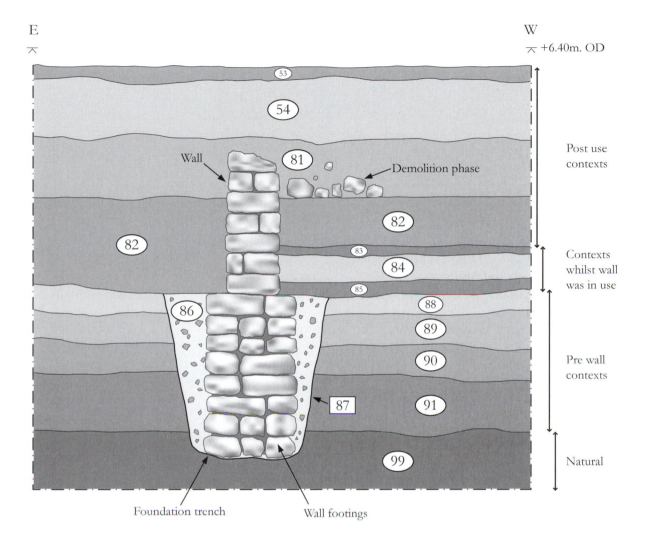

E   W   +6.40m. OD

53
54

Wall   81   Demolition phase   Post use contexts

82   82   Contexts whilst wall was in use

83
84
85

86   88

89

90

87   91   Pre wall contexts

99   Natural

Foundation trench   Wall footings

Fig 82 Excavation and dating of wall footings. It will be necessary to give context numbers to the wall itself, and the different phases of construction.

be sampled and a full photograph or photogrammetric survey done of the structure prior to removal.

Stone coursing

It may be necessary to describe the structure course by course and to use a new context number on obvious repairs and rebuilds. A note must be made on any inclusions found in the structure. In post-Roman walls and foundations these will include Roman building material and

any unusual stones or marble or sculpted fragments. It is advisable to dismantle the wall course by course, recording and planning any significant stone as it becomes visible. The harder stone tends to be on the outside of the building, with a softer stone on the inside that may also be plastered. If the stone is plastered, record where the rendering ends, as this may indicate floor levels or, if vertical, internal partition walls. If the stone is soft on both faces, and both faces are plastered, the wall is likely to be an internal wall. Any graffiti will need to be recorded on a 1:1 drawing, photographed and retained for study.

Any evidence of tools used on stone will need to

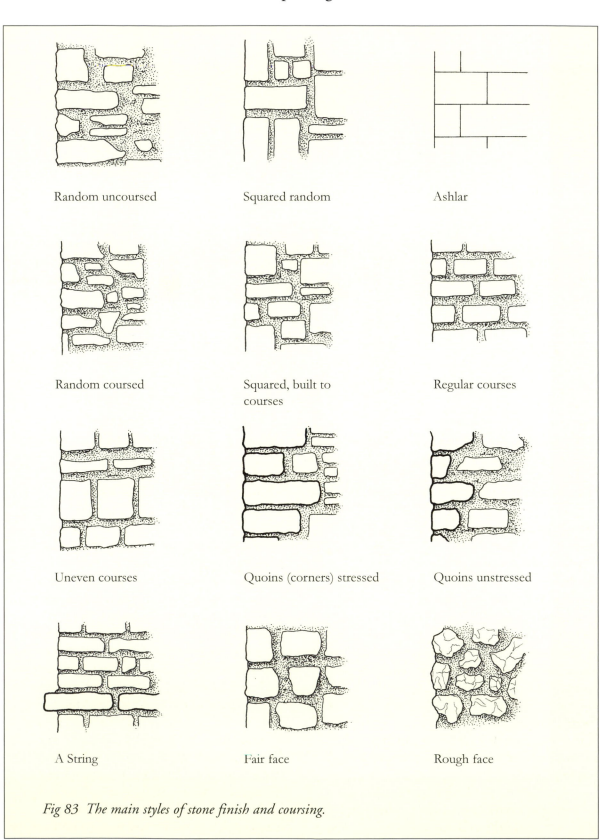

Random uncoursed

Squared random

Ashlar

Random coursed

Squared, built to
courses

Regular courses

Uneven courses

Quoins (corners) stressed

Quoins unstressed

A String

Fair face

Rough face

Fig 83 The main styles of stone finish and coursing.

be shown on the elevation drawings (at 1:10) and drawn at 1:1 or 1:5, depending on size. If retained, mark the top of the stone with a 'T' using a permanent black marker and mark elsewhere with a site code and context number.

Brickwork

Recording brickwork is in many aspects the same as that for any other type of solid building material. However, specialised terms are used for the laying of bricks, i.e. on bed, on edge and on end. Typical brick bonding patterns will include English, English Cross, English Garden Wall, Rat Trap, Flemish, Header, Stretcher, Herringbone and Lacing courses. The mortar bed on which the bricks are laid should be recorded.

Roman Mortar is usually pinkish, from numerous inclusions of tile flecks or brick dust, or orange from sand and gravel.

Saxon mortar is usually grey, of poor quality with few inclusions, whilst Early Medieval is orange/brown with a high sand content. Late Medieval has a high proportion of charcoal fleck and is light grey in colour. In brickwork the mortar is usually lime-based, and the pointing of the mortar between the bricks can give an indication of the type and appearance of the building.

The type of pointing used can indicate the external face of the building and the

Fig 84 The contrast between the thin Roman bricks and the eighteenth-century bricks is apparent in the fabric of St Martin's church in Canterbury. The later bricks have been used to repair the buttress of this Anglo-Saxon, or possibly Roman building mentioned by Bede.

contemporary ground level.

Recording timber and timber structures

In suitable environmental conditions wood can survive for thousands of years. It is essential to undertake detailed recording of timber structures as soon as they are exposed. Wood, once exposed to the open air, will tend to shrink and deteriorate unless kept wet. There are two aspects of recording timber: one is to record the structure, i.e. how the timber has been worked, and two, the environmental aspects of the timber as part of a tree in a growing wood. The enormous cost of preserving timber normally means that any found on excavations can rarely be preserved. The only exceptions are usually boats that are prehistoric or with known historical associations.

Because timber structures are rarely retained, it is important that they are recorded accurately and that a timber specialist be involved. It has been found on past excavations that parts of boats have been reused as quay revetments, well and pit linings, and the identity of these reused ships' timbers is the provenance of the specialist. The level of recording necessary can be seen in the Timber Recording Sheet used by the Museum of London. The Timber Recording Sheet will enable the timber to be recorded in its stratigraphic position, and to establish its shape as exposed by excavation. It should enable an isometric drawing to be done.

Dendrochronology is an absolute dating procedure carried out by specialists. If sufficient tree rings have survived, which must include up to the bark and the wood is oak, it is possible to find out the exact year of felling.

Oak trees are usually felled in the autumn and used green, so it is possible for structures using green oak to be dated within months, and of course any finds found in the same context can benefit from this absolute date.

To record timber the structure must have a general context number and a description recorded on a Timber Recording Sheet. This should record positioning, orientation, degree of survival and its stratification position. It will

Fig. 85 The main types of brick bonding

need to cross-refer to the numbers of all the individual timbers that are part of the structure, and record all the numbers of all drawings and photographs.

A note must be taken of how many dendrochronological samples were taken. Finally

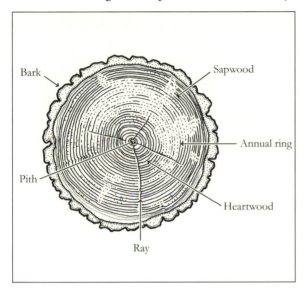

an interpretation should be made of the structure's possible function and history.

The structure will need to be drawn at 1:20 in plan and 1:10 in elevation and section. Separate timbers should be drawn at 1:10, whilst any tool tally or graffiti marks must be traced/drawn at 1:1 and photographed. All the drawings will need to indicate the direction of grain in the individual timbers and to show a timber cross-section displaying the conversion method and the degree of sapwood and bark survival.

The dendrochronological analysis of the samples taken will attempt to show what tree species were used, the age of the timber, how it was converted, i.e. squared, halved, quartered, and whether the planks are radially or tangentially faced. Photographs will show the three-dimensional aspect of the structure and provide step-by-step images of the diametric of the structure. Once the necessary recording has been accomplished, it may be possible to re-construct the structure as an isometric drawing.

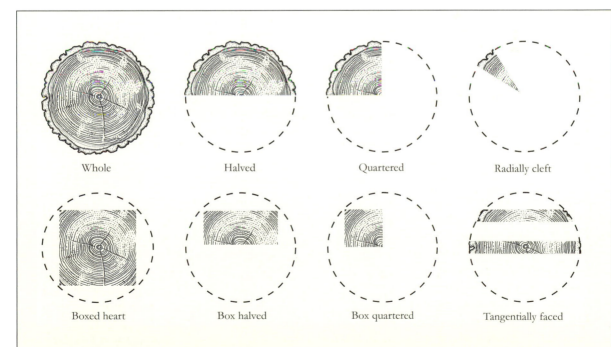

Fig. 86 The main types of timber conversion need to be recorded accurately, whether halved, quartered, radially cleft or boxed heart.

CHAPTER NINE: RECORDING SKELETONS

'**Scientific examination of human skeletons can provide information on the demography, diet, health and disease, growth, physical appearance, genetic relationships, activity patterns and funerary practices of our forebears**'
(Environmental Archaeology, English Heritage, 2002).

Excavated human remains should always be treated with respect and decency. If an excavation is expected to disturb human remains, a Section 25 Licence should be obtained from the Home Office (Tel 0207 035 5530). In the majority of cases excavated human remains pose no special health or safety risk, but medical specialists advise that people coming into contact with human remains of the 17th century and later should be inoculated against smallpox.

As with animal bones, soil acidity is an important determinant of human bone survival, with greater preservation being found in neutral or alkaline conditions. Work on human remains is an area where a number of important new techniques are available, in particular stable isotope and DNA analysis.

Recording skeletons and burials

It is essential here also to retain the Single Context Recording system, but also to record on the Skeleton Recording Sheet. The following specialists should be consulted prior to full excavation:

Historians. If the burials are later medieval or early modern it may be possible to consult burial registers or other records to assess the characteristics of the local population or working practices.

Human osteologist. It may be that the skeletons are not worth keeping for post-excavation research. This may influence the collection policy and the recording and excavation methods employed.

Environmental. An environmental specialist will need to be consulted about the viability of sampling deposits from burials. Sampling for parasites in the gut region is difficult and time consuming, but if it can be shown that the preservation of organic material is good then a controlled sampling procedure may be required. The Skeleton Recording Sheet, as used by the Museum of London, is the recommended model of its type.

Specialists recognise that photography is the best way of recording a skeleton in situ. It has been shown that site drawings of skeletons in situ at a 1:10 scale are often inaccurate, and photography is both rapid and accurate. However, it is essential to locate the photographed skeleton in relation to the site grid. To prepare a skeleton for photography, carefully clean the bones, apart from the hands and feet, which should be lifted as a block of soil. Start cleaning at the skull and work down towards the feet. If the bones are well preserved they can be cleaned with a small sponge and limited amounts of water. The skeleton should be photographed immediately the bones have been exposed and cleaned, making sure a suitable scale, cardinal point and skeleton number are visible on a white board.

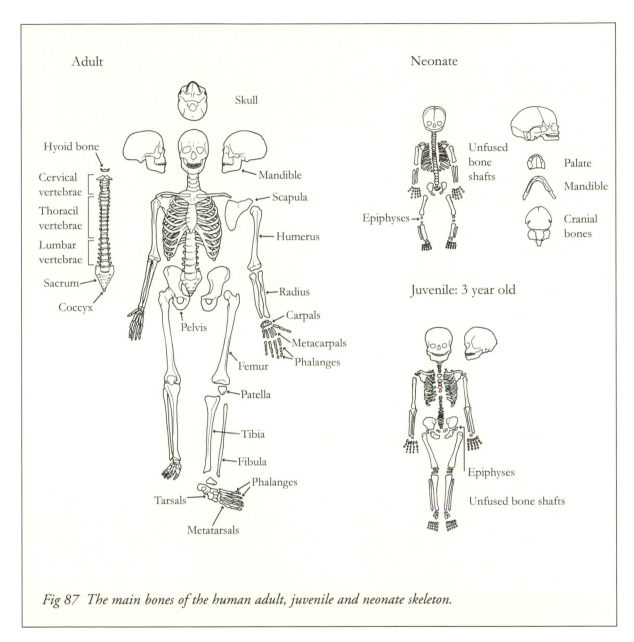

Fig 87 *The main bones of the human adult, juvenile and neonate skeleton.*

To record the location of the skeleton first draw its outline on the 1:20 plan of the grave cut. This is best achieved by drawing precisely the outlines of the skull, pelvis and long bones. At the post-excavation stage the drawing can be overlaid on the photograph and the rest of the bones drawn in. Another method to locate the skeleton in the drawn record is to place large-headed nails painted white at appropriate points around the skeleton. These can be planned in to the drawing by offset or triangulation and will show up on the vertical photograph. It will be necessary to record the vertical height of the burial, and levels will need to be taken on the highest and lowest parts of the skeleton and on the two ends, usually the highest points of the skull and feet. If individual grave goods are exposed during excavation they should be itemised with their levels and site grid co-ordinates, photographed and drawn in situ on a separate sheet and also drawn at a scale of 1:10 on the skeleton drawing.

Removal of the skeleton

The lifting, bagging and recording of a skeleton must be accomplished with care and respect, keeping in mind that the amount of information obtainable from a skeleton is directly related to how complete it is.

Remove and record the skeleton in this sequence.

1. Lift and bag the right hand and arm.
2. Repeat with the left arm and left hand.
3. Lift and bag the right leg and right foot.
4. Repeat with the left leg and left foot.
5. Wrap the skull in cling film if fragile, and do not pick it up by the eye sockets.
6. The torso, including pelvis and vertebrae, must be bagged up together.
7. Neonatal foetal skeletons should be block-lifted to ensure the maximum recovery of all the small bones.

Ensure that sufficient air is trapped in the bag to act as a cushion. Fold over the opening and staple shut.

Make sure a recording label is placed inside the bag and the same information is written on the outside. All skeleton bones are fragile. So ensure that you take great care in bagging and recording. Place inflated bags into a box as soon as feasible.

If a cremation is found in a complete pot, make sure that the pot is wrapped in cling film, bandaged, and removed in its entirety- for x-ray.

On no account allow pots to be emptied on site and the contents recorded separately. Ensure the excavator dry sieves (1cm mesh) any remaining fill of the grave to retrieve the smallest bones and other small artefacts for recording. It may be worthwhile to bag the soil for processing off site.

Fig 88 The human osteologist will decide on the collection policy of any given site by taking in the factors like number of skeletons, the state of preservation, date, range and method of burial.

Here, the skeleton of a young women is being prepared for photography prior to lifting by students of the KAFS. Damage has been caused to the skull by ploughing.

CHAPTER TEN: SOIL SAMPLING

'The main issues in environmental archaeology concern ecological, social and economic reconstruction' (*Environmental Archaeology, English Heritage, 2002*).

The nature of the past environment is of huge importance to archaeologists. How and where people lived were usually shaped by their environment. Thus the environmental remains will provide an insight into climate, the environment and ecological conditions.

Animal bones

Bones will last well in non-acidic soil, but it is usually only the hard tissues — bones, teeth, horn cores and antlers — that will survive. Soft tissues usually only survive in extreme climatic conditions by freezing or desiccation. The larger bones of animals are usually retrieved during excavation. Fine-mesh sieving (1mm) will be required to recover bird and fish bones, whilst the collection of larger animal bones can be made easier by using coarse-mesh sieving (see Fig 91). Bones should be carefully cleaned either by dry brushing or by using a little water. Animal bones can be used in a variety of studies, most of which aim to show how the presence of bones at an archaeological site relates to past human activities, beliefs and environment.

Although the use of DNA techniques is being developed to address these questions, the more traditional investigative methods, using analysis of skeletal size and shape, are beginning to show that regional and modern forms of domestic cattle and sheep developed much earlier than has been suggested by most of the recent documentary evidence.

Molluscs

The shells of both marine and land molluscs can be found preserved in many types of sediment, but they last particularly well in alkaline sediments which are not conducive to the survival of pollen grains. Some molluscs can be responsive to changes in the microclimate, but many species have a broad tolerance to change. The quality of preservation of the shells is the key to the identification of species, and it will be necessary to sieve in order to ensure the whole assemblage is retained for study.

Seeds and plant remains

Seeds need to be identified at species level. This can only be done by observing them under a microscope and, as with shells and bones, seeds will need to be compared with a reference collection. Retrieval in the field is by sieving using flotation techniques, which screen the material into the various categories.

Pollen analysis

As with all environmental samples collected from archaeological sites, the processing of pollen requires specialist knowledge and it is essential to involve environmental archaeologists from the very beginning of an archaeological project. Size, surface texture and shape are examined under a microscope that allows identification of family or of genes rather than species. However, recent advances in technology have made it possible to catalogue species. Pollen and spores are so small that they can be widely scattered from the parent plant by wind and rain. Thus, caution is required when interpreting the vegetation of an area. In naturally accumulated deposits, the pollen assemblage will provide an idea of the vegetation for some distance around the site.

Insects

Insects are characterised by having six legs and a segmented body and are the most diverse class of life on earth, outnumbering by far the number of plant species. Insects live in all of the world's ecosystems and are invaluable in reconstructing past environments. On rural sites insects are extremely useful for showing the character of woodland, the quality of water and the occurrence of domestic animals, whilst grain beetles can provide evidence of ancient grain storage.

Soils and sediments

Geoarchaeological work on site investigates both site formation processes and landscape changes. Geoarchaeology examines both soils and sediments. Past peoples can deposit sediment through activities such as terracing, building earthworks or levelling uneven surfaces. By studying soil and sediments, geoarchaeologists can inform archaeologists on the processes that have changed the stratigraphy, and formation of the archaeological site.

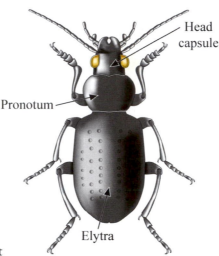

Fig 89 The Carabidae beetle showing the parts which usually survive in the archaeological record.

Examination of stratified deposits on site is the single most important method for studying site formation processes. A knowledge of sedimentation processes, weathering effects and soil formation has to be interwoven with the available cultural information to provide an integrated understanding of how the archaeological site was formed. Fieldwork is the most important aspect of any geoarchaeological study and the recording must be of the highest quality.

Colour and grain size

The first task of any description of soil or sediment is to define the colour. To standardise colour descriptions of sediments and soils it is essential to use a Munsell Soil Colour Chart.

This is a book that contains standard colour pallets, which can be directly compared to the soil or sediment in the field. Two colour determinations are usually required, one of dry and one of moist soil or sediment. The Munsell Soil Colour Chart defines the colour on the basis of hue, value and chroma. All geoarchaeologists use the Munsell Soil Colour Charts, and recording a colour on the basis of its Munsell number and description will enable those who read the report to understand immediately the colour of the soil.

Except for very coarse particles, the individual grains of soil are not actually measured but an estimate is based on a visual key (Fig 90), or by the 'feel' of the particles to an experienced geoarchaeologist. Once wet, a sediment or soil dominated by clay will easily smear when rubbed in the hand, whilst that dominated by silt will not. Grittiness means that sand is also present.

Sorting

Past peoples modified and mixed the stratigraphy of a site by processes of re-deposition. Pits, postholes and ditches are a common feature on archaeological sites. The materials removed from these features are usually dumped elsewhere on site and these newly formed deposits will probably be poorly sorted. This is because the mixture of source material is dumped unceremoniously and will include ceramic shards, bone and a variety of discarded debris. Therefore, when recording stratigraphy on an archaeological site, it is possible to separate deposits that formed from natural landscape processes from those that are the result of human activity.

Soil Sampling

Recovery and analysis

English Heritage guidelines for environmental samples are as follows:

Course-sieved samples: The sample size of a deposit is normally about 100 or more litres and should be of 'whole earth' with nothing removed unless it is so large and bulky as to interfere with the processing.

The samples may be sieved wet or dry, depending on the soil conditions, and are usually processed on site. The minimum mesh size is 2mm; coarse-sieved samples are often collected from deposits that are unusually rich in bone or shell and are best taken with the advice of the appropriate specialist.

Flotation samples: These are taken from well-drained deposits for the recovery of charred plant remains from the 'flot' and for charcoal fragments, small bones, mineralised plant remains and industrial residues such as hammer scale. Samples are placed on a 1mm or 500 microns mesh suspended in an oil-drum tank of water. The sediment rests on the mesh while the charred remains, being less dense than water, float to the surface. Water is then sprayed through the fine mesh from underneath, which increases the water level in the tank and enables the lighter charred particles to float. As the water level rises further it passes over the lip of the tank carrying with it the charred remains, which are then usually collected on a sieve with a mesh size of 250-300 microns. The charred material caught in the sieve is the flot, while the other material contained within the mesh inside the container is called the residue or heavy fraction. Nylon mesh is available from Northern Mesh and Technical Fabrics, Oldham, Manchester.

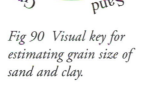

Fig 90 Visual key for estimating grain size of sand and clay.

The advice of an English Heritage specialist should be sought to establish the most appropriate mesh size for any given site.

Specialist samples

These are usually collected by specialists and processed off-site. Samples can include:

1. Large samples. These are normally in the order of 20 litres, and are collected from water-logged, anoxic deposits and usually provide plant and invertebrate macrofossils. The samples can be taken from individual contexts or from vertical sections.

2. Monolith samples. These are collected from vertical sections in monolith tins, squared plastic guttering or Kubiena boxes. Samples taken can be sub-sampled in the laboratory for a range of analysis, of pollen, spores and diatoms.

3. Cores. Cores can be taken for a range of materials similar to those in monolith samples and small samples.

4. Small samples. These are collected separately, from contexts, and will include certain material such as ostracods, marine molluscs, pollens and spores etc.

Taking samples

Samples should be taken from individual contexts, unless they are monolith samples that cross stratigraphic boundaries. Sometimes it is more appropriate to sample 'thick' contexts in spits of 5-10cm. All samples should be double bagged or collected in 10-litre plastic boxes available from English Heritage. Each sample must have two labels of plastic or plasticised paper marked with a permanent marker pen. Samples in poly bags should be double-bagged and a label placed inside the double bag facing out and the other attached to the top of the bag.

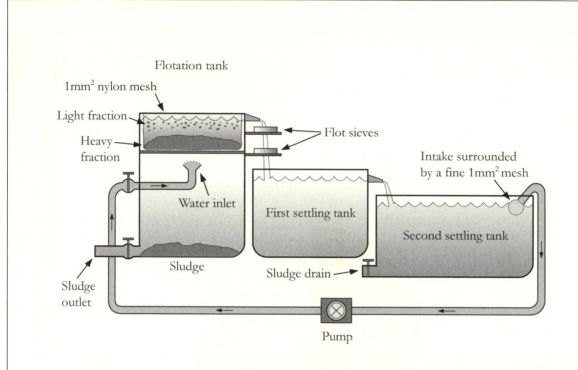

Flotation tank

1mm^2 nylon mesh

Light fraction

Heavy fraction

Flot sieves

Intake surrounded by a fine 1mm^2 mesh

Water inlet

First settling tank

Second settling tank

Sludge

Sludge drain

Sludge outlet

Pump

Fig 91 Plant recovery by water flotation. The system illustrated above was developed by Gordon Hillman and uses a flushing system utilising recycled water. The lighter material floats to the surface of the water and is collected in the flot sieves. The heavier material sinks down in the flotation tank and is caught by the nylon mesh.

Securely tie the outer bag with synthetic string; it is essential the bag is properly sealed to prevent the samples drying out or being contaminated by bacterial decay. Plastic boxes (each 10 litres) should be labelled twice on the inside and once on the outside. Labels should include: the site code, context number, context type and the sample number. Boxes of specialist samples, with an orientation preserved, such as cores, monoliths and Kubiena boxes, need to have the tops and bottoms of the samples marked and the depth within the sequence of the deposit recorded; overlapping samples must have their relationships recorded. The position of samples should be marked on all relevant site plans and section drawings. Specialists will usually make sketches and notes that should be incorporated in the site archive. Photographic records of the samples' sequence can be useful in providing a record of sample location and orientation.

Sample Recording Sheets

There are two types of Sample Recording Sheets. The soil sample sheet is to be used for sediment samples that require 'on-site' or laboratory processing. The other, the single-item sample sheet, is for recording spot finds, carbon-14 samples, dendrochronological samples and other items for identification, in addition to the sample sheets on the environmental sample register in which an account of the sample's context number and context description must be kept in the site archive.

The soil Sample Recording Sheets are similar in format to the general Recording Sheets and include information on the sizes of individual items in the sample, degree of contamination, inclusions, context type, and the percentage of the sample in relation to the whole context, the reason for sampling and the specific questions to be asked about the sample. The single-item sample sheet records any individual item or specific sample that requires identification. It will include the number of the sample, which will also be recorded in the Environmental Sample Register, any sub-samples, such as several slices of wood for dendrochronological dating, the sample type, and the type of feature. Samples will need to be indexed with the site code, area or trench number, context number, sample number, date, initials and also the number of the sample if several samples are taken from the same deposit. The sample number is written in a diamond.

Once retrieved from the field, samples should be processed immediately, but if this is not possible you should maintain samples in conditions as close as possible to those in the ground. They should be kept chilled and dark and stored in airtight containers. This will slow down bacterial and algal growth and will help in the preservation of the organic material. It is not usual to store unprocessed dry samples as they should be processed on site during the excavation and the results recorded on sample record forms to an agreed format.

Fig 92 The stratigraphy in the photograph of a ditch cut in the Roman period at Syndale in Kent, shows that the poorly sorted layers of the infill at the top of the ditch were deliberately deposited to level off the ditch. In contrast, the fine, well-sorted lower layers of the stratigraphy were formed during weathering of the open early Roman military ditch dated by pottery to the mid 1st century AD.

CHAPTER ELEVEN: SMALL FINDS

'Only in the last resort should a find be cut round to release it from the ground. Doing this destroys its relationship with unseen layers and may well obscure its real function, origin or derivation'
(Techniques of Archaeological Excavation, Philip Barker, 1982).

Finds provide both dating evidence and useful information about patterns of trade and the economic status of a site. The close relationship of finds to a well-recorded sequence of contexts that is easily accessible through the site archive, and ultimately the written report, is the cornerstone of modern archaeology. The term 'Terminus ante quem' can be used to define a relative chronological date to a deposit and if combined with 'Terminus post quem' the deposit can be dated securely between the two.

Usually a find, be it a small Roman coin or sherd of pottery, will appear whilst trowelling the surface of a context. The context will have its own unique number and the find can be labelled as coming from that context. However, a find may appear at the junction between two layers. It is usual to assign such finds to the upper, later layer rather than the one below, but it may be necessary to record the exact position of the find within the context. When cleaning sections, it is most important to record the exact position of a find, not only within its context but also on the section drawing.

It should be the site policy that all finds, however insignificant, should be recovered.

This may entail sieving for total recovery of small items and detecting for all metals. It is important that as much finds evidence as possible should be recovered and recorded for future researchers. Biased evidence can easily result from a selective recovery policy in the past. For example, the preferential collection of Samian ware — being bright red, it is highly visible — over other types of Roman pottery, has led to inaccurate inferences being made in subsequent reports.

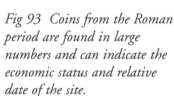

Fig 93 Coins from the Roman period are found in large numbers and can indicate the economic status and relative date of the site.

All finds should be treated with the utmost respect, and removed without the trowel touching them. Finds that have been lying in the soil for hundreds of years will have reached a more or less stable chemical and physical state until they are exposed to the environment by excavation; from that point deterioration will start.

If the find seems fragile, do not remove it from its matrix of earth, as field treatment may be necessary by the Site Conservator or English Heritage specialist. Check daily that damp or wet objects do not dry out while stored on site. Double bag; avoid handling. Store in a damp box. Do not separate components (e.g. shoes). Contact finds section if waterlogged deposits are encountered. Take individual finds to the finds section as soon as possible.

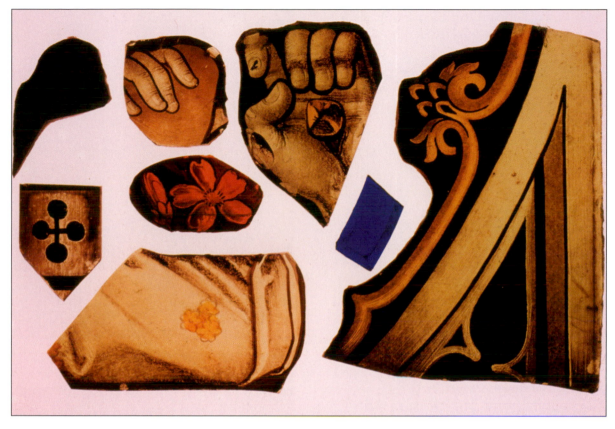

Fig 94 Stained-glass fragments retrieved through field-walking at Teynham by the KAFS indicate the importance of the site and the necessity of cataloguing small finds.

Recording finds

Finds usually fall into two categories; one category consists of pottery, bone, shell, flint and stone, which are common finds, and the other category is small finds, which are usually coins, brooches and other metalware, glass, whole or fragmented pots and decorated pottery.

Common finds

Common finds are usually bagged in material-specific categories, one bag for bone, one for pottery, one for building material etc. Write on the bag the site code, the context number, finder's initials, date and, if applicable, the find number drawn in an upright triangle.

Common finds are sometimes recorded in a find's index, although the Finds Specialist usually undertakes this task. The list may have to be material-specific, i.e. separate indices for pottery, bone, metal, worked stone etc.

Small finds

Finds of importance — coins, worked stone, glass, metalwork — need to be carefully recorded. On some research sites a particular type of find may need to be recorded in a separate finds category, and if deemed necessary recorded three dimensionally. The level of recording in a Small Finds Index would be:

1. The find number
2. Description
3. Context number
4. Area code
5. Co-ordinates and levels
6. Plan or section
7. Initials and date

Co-ordinates need to be measured from the site grid using offset or triangulation, whilst a site level from the TBM can measure the level. Most archaeologists record the small finds in a Small

Finds Index, and most will also use a Small Finds Sheet, which will include:

1. Context number
2. Small find's number
3. Object sketch (with dimensions)
4. Co-ordinates
5. Levels
6. Plan and section numbers
7. Photograph numbers
8. Method of excavation
9. Description
10. Excavator's name
11. Checked by and date

Until a specialist report is made, this will be the only descriptive record of the find. In the sketch, try and clarify the material of the object, and any distinguishing features. Some archaeologists will now digitally photograph the small find in the field and attach the colour print out to the Small Finds Sheet.

Waterlogged finds

Waterlogged deposits can be the most exciting and fruitful for excavators. The waterlogged environment is usually anaerobic, and so there is insufficient oxygen to support the bacteria that cause decay and for the oxidation of metals.

Unfortunately, as soon as organic and metallic objects are exposed to the air they will begin to deteriorate through oxidation and drying. Items such as worked leather, worked wood, cloth and organic material will need to be packed in an environment that is as close as possible to that from which they came.

Waterlogged finds can be double-packed in self-sealing bags, but they cannot be opened more than once or twice without losing their watertight properties. Once the waterlogged find is packed in a bag, add a waxed label between it and the next bag and write on the outside of the second bag the information required.
If using a white sample box, write the information needed on the lid and on an internal white plastic plant label.

Fig 95 Conservation starts in the field. Here a metal detectorist find of Iron Age swords and spears found in a pit lined with first century Roman pottery is being carefully unearthed by a conservator from the York Archaeological Trust.

The world famous 'Seahenge' found at Holme in Norfolk. Post-excavation work by Maisie Taylor and Peter Murphy tells us how the timber circle was constructed and what sort of landscape setting it was found in. Dendrochronology by Cathy Groves gives a construction date of 2049BC.

How to deal with finds

Make sure that the find is protected from damage. If possible lift it within its matrix of soil which can be removed by specialists later. Put the find in a sealable perforated polythene finds bag and make sure you write on the bag where the object was found, the date and its position in the field or co-ordinates if found on an archaeological site.

If the find has come from a wet or water-logged environment it is essential to keep the object wet and not to let it dry out. Store in a waterproof polythene bag and take to a conservator. If the site has waterlogged conditions it will be necessary to have a conservator on site. Metals (apart from gold) will corrode in the presence of water and air and revert to their natural mineral (or ore) forms. Each metal will behave differently.

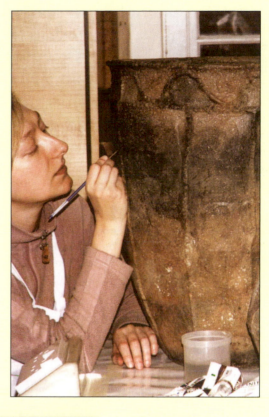

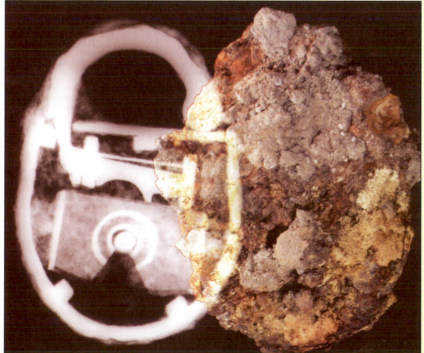

Fig 96 It can take up to 230 hours to conserve a large Bronze Age pot (above). Conservators have just finished a four-year project at the Salisbury and South Wiltshire Museum to save 105 Bronze Age ceramic pots.
The original Victorian conservators used a variety of materials including cement and bicycle spokes.
The x-ray of a post-medieval padlock as excavated and with the padlock mechanism revealed through x-ray.

CHAPTER TWELVE: WHAT NEXT?

'Archaeology depends upon a fragile and finite resource. It is the archaeologist's duty to conserve this resource and to make the results of a fieldwork project, including the original archive, available to the public'
(Unravelling the Landscape, Mark Bowden, 1999).

Philip Barker, writing in 1977, was very aware that excavation is destruction, and often total destruction, but also that evidence uncovered by excavation enables us 'by acts of sober imagination to recover fragmentary glimpses of the past, like clips of film from an old silent film, badly projected'. In Britain, large swathes of our landscape are being destroyed daily. The activity of field walking is based on the premise that the finding of sites is due to damage caused to the buried monument by the plough. Through planning procedures, the various agencies are able to catch some of this potential destruction, but in the countryside modern ploughing is destroying literally hundreds of sites each year. There can be nothing more soul-destroying than visiting a field recently ploughed and picking up hundreds of pieces of marble mosaic from a destroyed Roman building.

It is right and proper that these sites are fully excavated before the plough finally destroys them. However, it is essential that the results of excavation are published during the lifetime of the excavator. However excellent the recording procedure, publication is not an abstract activity based entirely on single-context recording sheets and small-finds indexes, or even the artefacts themselves. There is no doubt that the collating of the evidence, the crystallisation of the results and the physical writing of the report are very different activities from the fieldwork. It can take as many people hours to write the report as it did to dig the site in the first place.

It is essential that money and time for post-excavation, pre-publication work be planned from the outset. It is pointless and morally indefensible to excavate without full publication of the results.

There are many ways to get your work published, there are local society reports, county journals, site monographs, special interest societies and even through a web site. Ensure that from the outset you talk to and involve people who will be interested in your work , and work to a Research Design which has been circulated and commented on by other archaeologists.

Fig 97 The future of archaeology is in the hands of the public. Archaeology must not just be for the 'archaeological elite'- it must reach out and involve people from all walks of life who, with their own expertise can bring their own contribution to the discipline. Here, (right and below left) a solicitor, civil servant and school teacher are actively recording our archaeological heritage.

Fig 98 The archaeologists of the future are of course the young. Training courses and Activity Days are organised by most of the large archaeological organisations. Here, (left) Museum of London archaeologists are showing children the potential excitement of an archaeological activity. The Young Archaeologists Clubs organised by the Council of British Archaeology (CBA) is a tremendous idea to involve the young in archaeology, and of course 'Time Team' is a household word on showing how to involve the public in archaeology.

Suggested Reading

Suggested reading

It would have been impossible to write this book without reference to:

Philip Barker, 1982, Techniques of Archaeological Excavation

F. Bettes, 1992, Surveying for Archaeologists

Mark Bowden, 1999, Unravelling the Landscape

Mark Bowden, 2002, With Alidade and Tape

The British Academy, 1999, Aerial Survey for Archaeology

J. Collis, 2001, Digging up the Past

Andrews K. & Doonan R., 2003, Test tubes & Trowels

P. Drewett, 1999, Field Archaeology: An Introduction

J. M. Hawker, 2003, Archaeological Field Recording

J. M. Hawker, 2003, Archaeological Field Drawing

English Heritage, 2002, Human Bones from Archaeological Sites

English Heritage, 2002, Environmental Archaeology

English Heritage, 2003, Where on Earth are We?

English Heritage, 2006, Guidelines on the X-radiography of archaeological metalwork

MOLAS, 1994, Archaeological Site Manual

T. Robinson & M. Aston, 2002, Archaeology is Rubbish

K. Wilkinson and C. Stevens, 2003, Environmental Archaeology

A1 Equipment Catalogue, 2003

York Survey Supply Catalogue, 2003

Index

Index

Index

Index

Picture Credits